HURRY BEFORE SUNDOWN

The Urgency of Evangelizing Our Nation

William G. Tanner

BROADMAN PRESS
NASHVILLE, TENNESSEE

4263-27
ISBN: 0-8054-6327-5

Dewey Decimal Classification: 266.122
Subject heading: MISSIONS, HOME
Library of Congress Catalog Card Number: 81-67205
Printed in the United States of America

This book is dedicated to the three lovely ladies
in my life: Mrs. Kyle Yates, Sr., Ellen Tanner,
and our delightful teenage daughter, Kim Tanner.

Contents

Foreword

A number of years ago when I heard that Dr. William Tanner was to be nominated as executive director of the Home Mission Board, I was delighted. The Tanners and the Cothens went to dinner to talk about the challenges and problems we would face together. We talked about cooperation between the agencies—the commonality of the missions of the boards, the overwhelming challenge of a lost nation and millions of individuals.

It was clear then and consistently has been since that Bill Tanner had lost people on his heart. Behind his smiling face is the sharp mind of an incisive thinker. Beyond his endless good humor is a firm and deep commitment to the idea that "the gospel is the power of God to salvation to everyone that believeth." Whenever he stands to speak, he is reminding us that America needs Christ.

In this volume you will feel his heart; you will see the functioning of his fine mind; and you will know who he is and what he is about.

His thought processes run deeper than most. His formulations of truth are usually not run of the mill. He uses a little different approach from most of us. Thus, he is fresh and sometimes provocative. Many times when I have heard him I have thought *I wish I had said that.*

Tanner brings to Southern Baptist life an unusually good and varied background. He earned the terminal degree in theology and another in educational administration. He has been the successful pastor of some fine churches. He has been president of two Baptist colleges and was successful in both.

He is my friend and colleague. One of his great strengths is that he had the good fortune to marry Ellen Yates.

It is a pleasure to commend to you this book on an important subject by a man who knows his field.

Grady C. Cothen
President
Baptist Sunday School Board

Preface

Job said, "Oh, that my words were written in a book." Since becoming a mission executive five years ago, I have been using a lot of words about missions. I have been preaching to people in their churches, to state and associational mission leaders, and talking to our missionaries from American Samoa to Puerto Rico and from the Florida Keys to the Arctic Circle. I have discovered that it is much easier to preach and talk than it is to write. I appreciate Broadman Press "writing my words in a book."

Hurry Before Sundown comes from the title of chapter 1. Jesus Christ is our exemplar and example for missions. He was driven by the relentless imperative of the Father's will and by his love for the Father. There is an urgency about our mission responsibility that I am not sure we are feeling. This book is sent with the prayer that we may all feel the urgency of the task of evangelizing our nation.

This book is about missions. It is not just about home missions. One cannot write about the mission challenges in the United States without thinking about taking the gospel to the ends of the earth. In both speaking and writing about missions I have not been able to get away from the inspiring and heroic 3,000 missionaries of the Home Mission Board. There are no more isolated and lonely places to serve anywhere in the world than some of our missions on Indian reservations, or in Alaska, or in inner-city Chicago. The commitment of these missionaries to Jesus Christ is unmatched by any missionaries who have ever been sent by any mission agency.

I have not always been a mission agency executive. I have been an educator. I have been a pastor of churches, and I still love my role as a preacher. Most of the content of this book was preached before it was written. The chapters really existed first as sermon manuscripts. I think the reader will detect that, which hopefully will be a strength of this book. When the message in this book was preached, many responded, giving their hearts to Christ or making a commitment to missions either as a career or voluntary missionary. I owe a great deal to my friend John Havlik in the Evangelism Section of the Home Mission Board for working with me to translate the spoken word into a readable style. I pray that the words will lose none of their power to convict and convert in this new medium of communication.

In the chapters of this book I have had in mind some of the crises that face us in our home mission task. "The Einstein Factor" defines the task of missions in taking the gospel to the ends of the earth until the end of time. "Our Mission to America" focuses on our own nation as a great mission opportunity. "Love, the Heartbeat of Home Missions" focuses on love as an important factor in the message and mission of the church. "Go Quickly and Tell" illustrates the urgency of the mission task of the church, using four women in missions as parables of missionary concern and commitment. "Hurry Before Sundown" personalizes the urgency of the missionary responsibility for the believer and the church.

I did not cross Jordan alone in the writing of this book. For the original sermon manuscripts and the manuscript of this book I am deeply indebted to *Missions USA* and other Home Mission Board materials for facts, illustrations, missionary stories, and so forth. My leadership in a very dynamic mission agency and the content of this book would have been impossible except for the staff of the Home Mission Board and their relationships to our missionaries.

I think this missionary book will prove to be useful to pastors seeking assistance in the preparation of missionary sermons.

Church mission study groups may well find this book a useful tool in educating church members for the missionary task. Church libraries may find it to be a useful tool to make available to individuals and groups interested in missions. Woman's Missionary groups and Baptist Men's organizations in the church may use it as a basis for programs, discussion groups, and seminar studies.

I share this book with my readers with a prayer that we will evangelize this nation before the year AD 2000. That is still my dream and my vision. To give every person the chance to hear the gospel at least once and to have the opportunity to respond and to give every person the possibility of becoming a part of a New Testament church within their community are biblical and challenging goals. If this book directs only a few ounces of my moral and spiritual weight on the side of reaching those goals, I will be very pleased and blessed.

WILLIAM G. TANNER
Atlanta, Georgia

1

Hurry Before Sundown

I can still hear my father saying to me, "Hurry and get home before sundown." In those days the fears were not the same as today. Today our fears are not rural fears of becoming lost in the woods, but fears of the city—the mugger and the rapist. Quite often Ellen says that she is going out and I say, "Get home before dark." In the Gospel of the holy hurry, Mark must have been thinking of "hurry before sundown" when he used the word *immediately* more times than all the other Gospel writers. He was in such a holy hurry to tell about Jesus Christ that he skipped the birth records, the baptism, and the temptation of Jesus in order to tell us about what he did in healing the sick, raising the dead, and preaching the gospel. Mark caught the spirit of the urgency of Jesus more than any of the other evangelists. Mark remembered that on one occasion Peter and the others were looking for Jesus and when they found him they told him, "Everyone is looking for you." He said to them, "Let us go somewhere else to the towns, nearby, in order that I may preach there also; for that is what I came out for" (1:38).

John also remembered Jesus saying, "Hurry before sundown," when he reported the healing of the man born blind. Jesus says, "We must work the works of Him who sent Me, as long as it is day; night is coming, when no man can work" (9:4). Jesus was driven by the relentless imperative of the Father's command, pressed by the compelling necessity of the Father's will, and moved by the overwhelming compulsion of the Father's love. Feeling deeply the lostness of humanity, responding urgently to death and disease, caring divinely about human pain

13

and suffering, loving constantly the faithless and fallen, he spent his days in unending toil and his nights in ceaseless prayer.[1]

Is there reason for us to "hurry before sundown"? Is there a reason for us to work while it is still day? Lost, one planet—a fallen sister of the stars—and billions of people are still on it. Lost, one nation, a nation under God, in an ocean of materialism, captainless, rudderless, drifting into the storms of confusion just off the reefs of destruction. Lost—man is overboard in a sea of space—and the man is Everyman. Lost, the faith of our fathers in a bottomless pit of doubt and skepticism. Lost, late last night somewhere near a mushroom cloud up Megaton Street, a man lost in the false hopes of scientism. Lost, a corporation executive in the killing pace for progress and the runaway race for status. Lost, a whole generation carried out to the sea of hedonism, in a leaky craft called "anomie." Lost, a million youth in the wilderness of secularism with no compass of authority and no water of life. Lost, mankind last seen somewhere outside Eden. There is good reason to hurry before sundown.

With Jesus it was always the next town, the next man, the next sinner. The lost, the unevangelized, and those who never heard constantly beckoned him on. There was always that nemesis, the shadow of the cross, telling him to hurry. Time is energy; we ought to conserve it. Time is money; we ought to invest it. Time is the stuff out of which life is made, and to waste it is sin. Are we really in a hurry to evangelize our nation? How many of us can confess one sleepless night or one toil-filled day in the last three months in the interest of a nation that is spiritually lost? How long has it been since we have put off important visitors with the reply, "There is no time to see you, we must go to the next town."

This imperative of immediacy concerning the evangelization of our nation is the one missing ingredient in our efforts to be on bold mission. We cannot argue the lack of resources with 35,000 churches, 13 million adherents, and a denominational unity that is the envy of the Christian world. Can our church, our association, our state, and our Convention claim urgency when it takes thirty-five of us to bring one person to Christ? Can we claim urgency when almost one half of our membership is nonresident, inactive, and for purposes of mission nonexistent? Can we claim urgency when we have lived so long with sliding statistics that we no longer bother to offer excuses? Can we claim urgency when our gains in giving represent the inflationary spiral more than sacrificial generosity? Can we claim urgency when we give more money every year in interest to bankers than we do to all mission causes? Your heart and mind both say no to these rhetorical questions.

We are not like our Lord in the "nowness" of our commitment to evangelize and congregationalize this nation. He was eager and we are reluctant. He was zealous and we are apathetic. He was enthusiastic and we are unresponsive. He filled days with the endless toil of preaching, teaching, and healing. He filled nights with ceaseless prevailing prayer to the Father. We fill our days with chasing financial security and our nights with *Love Boat, Fantasy Island,* and *Saturday Night Live.* Winston Churchill in his great speech to beleaguered Britain said of the Royal Air Force, "Never did so many owe so much to so few." May it not be said of our missionary zeal, "Never did so many miss so much because, of all the millions of Christians, there were too few who would pay the price." Only a few of us know the peace of holy living. Only a few of us know the joy of sacrificial giving. Only a few of us know the thrill of bold witnessing.

Paul urges the Ephesians to "learn Christ." This chapter is an appeal to Christlikeness in our mission urgency. We cannot be Christ, but we can be like him. The very name by which we are known is "Christian," and it means "Christlike." How long will we wait while the harvest rots in the field? How long will we continue to offer our lame excuses while he continues to say to us, "The harvest is ripe and the laborers are few"? How long before we see through his eyes the unevangelized, the unloved and unloving who wait for missionaries that never come, for preachers who never will preach, and for churches that will never be started? How long will we enjoy our flowery beds of ease when our Lord who never promised us a rose garden beckons us on and urges us to hurry before sundown.

The moment is ours. We are now standing in the beginning of two critical decades in the history of this nation. They are decades that will usher in the third millennium since our Lord was here. They are decades when our nation trembles on the thin edge between greatness and decay. They are decades when our denomination will decide whether it is to be a people of destiny and purpose or a people afflicted with spiritual senility whose theme song is "old rockin' chairs done got me." This is a time when we must exhibit in our sacrifice, our servanthood, and our service the exciting reconciling awareness that Jesus Christ is alive. Moses said to Israel, "See, I have set before thee this day life and good, and death and evil" (Deut. 30:15, KJV). Our choice is exactly that. Life and good are all wrapped up in being the people of God on mission in God's world. Death and evil are epitomized in becoming a fractured, divisive, narrow people sensitive only to self-preservation.

Three words characterize the Jesus of Mark's Gospel. They are words that are crowned with crisis, intense with immediacy, pregnant with purpose, and heavy with hurry. The first of the words is "urgency," and it relates to people who were the first concern of Jesus. The religious leaders specialized in institutions. Jesus specialized in people. The second word is "emergency," and it relates to the relentlessness of passing opportunity. Jesus moved and was constantly moved as if time were running out. The third word is "fervency," and it relates to the spirit and quality of response. The disciples noted his zeal and quoted the Old Testament to support what they saw in him (Ps. 69:9; John 2:17). The Greek root for *zeal* is "to boil" (*Zeo*), and he literally boiled with fervency. He lived in the spirit and faith of the psalmist whose zeal for the will and word of God literally consumed him (Ps. 119:139).

The Urgency of People

Urgency cannot be put into the sibilant hiss of the computer tapes. Urgency cannot be compressed into the orderly columns of statistical tables. Urgency cannot be extrapolated in terms of dollars and cents. Urgency cannot be exposited in terms of countries, nations, counties, or cities. Urgency cannot be communicated in terms of ethnic, cultural, and social barriers. Urgency can only be expressed in terms of John, Mary, Hosea, Carmelita, Samuel, Rebecca, Hans, and Gertrude. Urgency now as in the days of our Lord is set to the music of compassion in the frothing mouth of the epileptic child down the street, the hungry babies in the ghetto on the other side of the tracks, the retarded child across the street, the drug addict stoned in an alley five blocks from our office, the teenage prostitute cruising the streets, and the spiritually poverty-stricken executive in a plush office across the hall. The urgency then is not geography or dollars, or counties or cities, but people. The urgency is not our self-survival to save America or our denomination, or ourselves, or our culture. It is people.

In Mark 1 our Lord began the mission to evangelize the world by opening a peripatetic clinic for the sick and suffering. He established a walk-in emergency room for the people. It was a clinic that specialized in training clinicians. The curriculum in his school was Compassion 101, Compassion 102, and Compassion 103. The graduate school specialized in compassion. The method of instruction was not lecture but laboratory. He showed his pupils the ulcerated sores of leprosy and said to them, "Touch him." He showed them how to take an epileptic in their arms and comfort him until the mouth frothed no more and the writhing limbs were quiet and supple. He lifted the limp limbs of the paralytic and showed them the tragedy of uselessness. He showed them all this and said, "This is the world and this is what's wrong with it. These are only the outward symptoms of the sickness unto death that we are come to cure. Before you can heal them you must love them. There is a sickness that I can't show you that is worse than death. Do not be afraid of these diseases that can kill the body, but be afraid of that sickness that can throw both body and soul into hell." Having finished their basic training, he immediately launched his campaign of world evangelization. We can imagine hearing him say once more to his men, "Let's hurry before sundown."

We have domesticated Jesus Christ.[2] We have chained him within stained-glass windows and imprisoned him in organ preludes. He was always free in the streets, but we have safely shut him up in church. He was always comfortable dining with sinners and saving prostitutes, but we have closeted him with the comfortable and the nice people. He was ever in the marketplace, but we have kept him out of the channels of commerce. He was always ready to talk about righteousness, love, and compassion, but we have barred him from the halls of justice. He preferred to start with demons and darkness and devils, but we have limited him to ladies' sewing circles and dilettante theological discussions. He loved to see sin wither and die when he passed by, but we want to keep him from pornographic bookstores, the houses of prostitution, and the ghettos of alienation and despair. He lived in the center of the controversies of life, but we make him the subject of rounds of philosophical discussions. He was a prophet who laid truth bare, but we have made him a rubber stamp for denominational programs and prejudices.

He stands outside our door and knocks, but we have forced him to peer through slatted windows into the tiny compartments of our lives, never bothering to open the door so he can roam the whole dwelling of our existence. Before we can loose him in the world, we will have to loose him in our lives. The night is coming. The urgency is real. The lost are waiting for the message. He stands and knocks, waiting to come in and to set us free from ourselves to be his ministers to people. He waits, and the people wait for us to set Christ loose in our lives so he can be set free in his world. The problem for all of us is not social or denominational or communal, but personal. We cannot keep trying to solve *our* problem until we solve *my* problem. My problem and yours is living our lives and opening our well-swept parlor to him but shutting him out of all those rooms marked business, pleasure, sex, marital relations, and prejudices and all those little secret closets hiding those darling sins.

Have we felt the urgency of people in our community, our nation, and the world? Have we responded to that urgency with instant obedience? I think we can safely say that we have not. We are living so insulated from the world around us in walls that are soundproofed by "what we shall eat, what we shall drink, and what we shall be clothed with." We are so insulated that we can no longer hear the crying of hungry babies, the complaints of the poor, and the anguish of the forsaken, forgotten, and unforgiven. Surrounded by our plastic gods, we are secure from the weather, our neighbors, and even our faith. We no longer need to worry about our destiny; we manufacture it and sell it in packaged splendor. What we don't have "how to" books for, we have pills for. "Downers" and "uppers" are readily available for "highs" or "lows" depending on our mood for the day. When nothing else works, we can get a high on readily available sex with no questions asked. We even have a pill to take away the guilt for that.

We are also incurably religious. We have even devised an evangelical faith for our brave new world. It is very religious, very chic, and very mystical. It features glossolalia, faith healing, and a religious superstar. We get our religious jollies out of the tube. The very excellent thing about getting your evangelical kicks out of the tube is that the tube never asks you to teach a Sunday School class or take care of a bunch of runny-nosed kids in the nursery. You don't ever worry about what would happen if the churches were all closed and the Sunday Schools out of business because you have your evangelical guru assuring you that he or she was a worldwide missionary enterprise. It is true that they ask you for money and it is money for which you or no one else ever receives an accounting, but it is so easy. That new evangelical faith for "born again" television disciples is as highly mobile as you are. It may be on a different channel in the next city, but it is the same voice, the same slick gospel salesman, and it is so wonderful that you didn't even have to move your membership. When the daughter gets married, you ask for the use of the local pastor and the local church, and you never even wonder that the church would not even be there if everyone supported it as you do. You even got a little angry when they charged you $25 for cleaning the church because you were not a member. "Don't they know that I am a born-again Christian?" you asked.

The good thing about this highly privatized, highly mobile religion is that you do not have to feel the urgency for evangelizing your community or nation because the urgency is satisfied in meeting the needs of the radio preacher for the "urgent need now" for a tent, or evangelizing the nation, or a project for overseas orphans. You never know how much of the money got there, but that doesn't worry you because meeting that urgent financial need made you feel so good. It is a world of money, machines, and media and "Isn't it wonderful that evangelical religion is keeping pace with the times." What can we say about this to a Lord who came and showed us how to teach children, how to reach men that are lost, and how to meet personally the spiritual challenge of our neighbor's lostness, brokenness, and alienation?

But we are not without our anxieties, our guilt, and our frustration in our brave new world. There are questions about the validity and worthwhileness of our life-style. Something seems to be missing at the very core of life. The creature comforts, the gadgets, do not give life the dimensions of faith, hope, and love. Life that is mechanized, corporate, noisy, and fast-moving doesn't give us identity and integrity. We do not feel human in the age of robots. Instant food, the commuter flight, and credit cards make us incapable of enjoying the beauty of a flower, the glory of a sunset, and the exquisite detail of a great painting. He invites us to come out of all of that and live lives of joy and peace, holiness and compassion, faith and responsibility through redemptive encounters with him and with our fellow human beings.

Can you feel the gut-twisting, mind-blowing, heart-rending urgency for the people of this land? Can you feel the pull of the people from the Florida Keys to Alaska's North Slope, from American Samoa to Puerto Rico—millions of square miles of wall-to-wall people? Do they cry out to you with the urgency of a Mayday, a tornado warning, or a hurricane alert? Our mission to America is not urgently spelled out for us in terms of money, programs, under-evangelized cities, or unchurched communities, but in terms of people—people that Christ loved and loves—people for whom he died. No, urgency is not found in graphs, infrastructured strength, progress charts, and success symbols. Urgency is written in the blue-black bruises on the body of a battered child in Phoenix. Urgency is fleshed out in the painted face of a teenage prostitute cruising on Tenth and Peachtree. Urgency is distilled in the killing loneliness of an aged couple in Miami waiting for letters that never come and phone calls that are never placed. Urgency is vocalized in the withdrawal screams of an addict in Chicago without enough bread for his next fix. Urgency is incarnate in a young man in Oakland whose search for a job ended in frustration and who now stands over the body of a convenience store operator with a smoking handgun. Urgency is etched in the face of a young mother in Dallas—no lights, no water, no heat, and her man long gone. See them? Hear them? Feel them?

> Sudden before my inward open vision
> Millions of faces crowded up to view;
> Sad eyes that said, "For us there is no provision.
> Give us your Savior too.
> "Give us," they cry, "your cup of consolation
> That never to our outstretched hands is passed.
> We long to know your Savior
> And oh, we die so fast."

Against the background of that bloody cross on a hill far away, need we ask a reason for the urgent need for our growing, giving, and going? The urgency of the needs of people demands our growing into his image as witnessing believers now. The urgency of the tragedy of human sin urges us to give ourselves and our life's possessions now. The urgency of my neighbor's lostness urges us to go to the ends of this nation with the gospel now. Delay is deadly to his mission; procrastination will paralyze his purposes. He says the mission is urgent. The Bible says the mission is urgent. Death tells us the mission is urgent. Hell makes the mission urgent. Compassion demands that the mission be urgent. Dare we wait any longer? Can we put off any longer the matter of taking our commission to evangelize this nation seriously?

The Emergency of Time

Time is the fabric out of which life is built. Time is relentless. Time is history. There is a mystery in time. Only now are we discovering its potential as the fourth dimension of physics. Time has the power to swallow up everything. The glory that once was Rome, the beauty of the hanging gardens of Babylon, the unimaginable awesome colossus at Rhodes are all swallowed up in time. The egomania of Hitler and Mussolini, the arrogance of Napoleon, the bloody hands of Stalin are all swallowed up in time. Time also has the power to drive us to a goal. Alexander was driven by his goal to conquer the world by military power. We have goals for ourselves such as so much money in savings for retirement by such and such a time. Time has the capacity to receive eternity. The new interest in time as the fourth dimension has made possible the concept of eternity in the black holes of space. The Bible says that the Creator has set eternity in our hearts.

If time drives us to make money, work hard, and commit ourselves to goals, it surely ought to give us a sense of emergency— time for us is running out. Time to evangelize the burgeoning multitudes of new immigrants is running out. Time to enter underevangelized counties is running out. Time to reenter the inner cities that we have forsaken is running out. Time is running out for us in both the personal and corporate dimensions. As a person you have only so much time left. Only so much time to invest in treasures in heaven where moth and rust cannot corrupt nor thieves break through and steal. Only so much time to evangelize your friends and neighbors. Time is running out for us as a denomination. Denominations that do not experience a renewal grow old and fossilize. That can happen to us. In the forties when we were in such a danger and baptismal ratios had hit new lows, we were challenged by new frontiers at the Convention in San Antonio. Our denomination experienced renewal, and, with a new lease on life, we experienced the greatest era of growth any denomination in modern times has experienced. We must feel the emergency of time running out for the new frontiers of the cities, the family, and the religious and ethnic minorities in America.

The New Testament is crystal clear in the fact that time impinges upon the present emergency from two directions. The church is under compulsion to evangelize and congregationalize this nation to its last lost individual and to its last churchless community. We are driven by the compulsion of geography. The church is to go to the ends of the earth. In relation to our mission to America our mission is to go and tell from Western Samoa on the west to Puerto Rico on the east, and from the Bering Sea on the north to the Florida Keys on the south. We cannot weasel out of this obligation. We cannot plead the lack of funds or the need for more time. The spiritual crisis is now. Acts 1:8-11 makes the geography of missions clear.

The church is under the second compulsion of the return of our Lord. The question of the angel of the ascension is still the burning question for the church: "Why stand ye there gazing?" The message is to occupy until he comes. The church is driven to the ends of the earth and to the end of time. It is unfortunate that we do not see the doctrine of the second coming in its missionary focus. While we are speculating about who the Antichrist is and what the mark of the beast is, the world rushes toward its date with the last judgment, and so many of the Christless have never heard. "Hurry before sundown" takes on new meaning in this context. A serious study of the missionary message of the New Testament reveals the second coming as the primary motivation for missions and evangelism. The emergency is the emergency of the unfinished task and the relentless march of time. If we want to talk about ages from the standpoint of the divine economy of all things, this is the age of missions. The interval between the resurrection of our Lord and his second coming in the clouds of heaven in great glory is the interval of world evangelization.

We dare not frame this emergency only in corporate terms for a denomination or a generation of believers. It must be framed in personal terms for you and me. This is our emergency. Time is running out for you, for your relatives, and your neighborhood. Time is running out for many that you meet in the regular traffic pattern of your life. The entire world in five hours knew about the tragic death of a thousand people in remote Guyana. But we cannot seem to get the message out to 13,000,000 Southern Baptists that millions who have never heard are dying without Christ. And this is not just happening in some remote primitive tribe, but in Milwaukee and Menominee, in Atlanta and Adel, in Miami and Mariana, in Minneapolis and Moose Lake. It is happening in your community and mine. It is not our inability to transmit news but our refusal to transmit good news that is so tragic. Every Christian is called upon to be a transmitter of the good news. There are no exemptions in his service. The situation is all the more tragic when we remember that he did not draft us, we volunteered. We wanted his salvation, his forgiveness, his peace, and his love. We have refused his mission, his task, his venture. One thing is certain and that is that every one of us has a date with him at the judgment seat of Christ to give an account of our missionary evangelistic stewardship.

Roy McClain has very clearly stated, "Encourage a sense of urgency about the task. Sitting until morning may be too late."[3] Jesus knew that there were some things that just couldn't wait. Every time we sit together at the Lord's table we are reminded,

"Proclaim the Lord's death until he comes." He promised us that he would eat of that supper with the twelve and us in the Kingdom. I have an idea that may be more of a checkup meeting than anything else. What did we do with that last dying command to go to the ends of the earth until the end of time? That question may be almost as embarrassing for us as that first Last Supper was for the betrayer. Our denomination has been saying a lot about Bold Mission. This has been the banner under which the Home Mission Board has been operating for several years. I am persuaded that Bold Mission will never be purposeful until it becomes personal.

The amazing spread of the Christian faith was and is a direct result of the invitation to the empty tomb, "Come and see," always being followed with the imperative command to "Go and tell." Missions is not man's scheme for influencing the world but God's purpose and plan for redeeming it. Whatever you may deem the time to be, this is no time for a "bailout" or a "freak out." There are those who believe that we are on the verge of a great spiritual revival. There are others who think we are facing very difficult times into the third millennium. No matter who is proven correct by history, our task is clear. We must evangelize whether it is popular or not. We must evangelize whether it fits the contemporary mood or not. We must evangelize whether it is difficult or easy. To tell every man the good news and plant churches where there are none is our task. We must hurry before sundown.

During a visit to the Soviet Union, our Baptist pastor guide explained to me and those in our group that the Communist Party maintains strict discipline in the lives of its members. It is only by strict discipline that they are able to control the daily lives and life-styles of a population of 300 million people. The thought immediately occurred to me that we as Southern Baptists had just reached 13 million members. I began thinking, *If 13 million Communists can seize control of 300 million lives by strict discipline and political power, could Southern Baptists, using spiritual power and strict discipline, influence the morality, ethics, and spiritual loyalties of millions in the United States?* Isn't discipline itself the very meaning of the word *disciple?* I spent much of the remainder of my trip wondering why Southern Baptists, 13 million strong, had not made more of an imprint on the life of this nation under God. Out of this a searching and devastating question evolves. Is it possible that one day we shall stand before the One who bears the print of nails in his hands and confess to our eternal shame that we lost several generations of the people of this land not because we were outnumbered but because we were outcommitted?

The Fervency of Our Response

The word *fervency* relates to the quality of our response. The word *fervency* communicates warmth, enthusiasm, zeal, and emotion. It is not enough to just respond to the mandate of our Savior and the needs of people. How we respond spells failure or victory. The root of the Greek word for zeal is *zeo* and it means "to burn" or "to glow." It is wonderful to go, and grow, and give, but not everyone can do those things with "glow." Simon Peter writes in his first epistle that "above all things" they are to be "fervent in their love." They are to be glowingly enthusiastic. It is also interesting that the word *enthusiastic* has its roots in a phrase "in the gods" that was used for the ecstatic worship of the Greek mysteries. In a series of lectures at Southern Seminary, Dr. Mackay, then president of Princeton said, "I can forgive a young pastor for anything except a lack of enthusiasm for the gospel he preaches." The same can be said for every Christian. We need fervency in evangelizing every community and fervency in taking the gospel to every person in this land.

Our loyalty to the missionary task of the church must come to us not as a reaction to grass-roots pressure nor as an effective tool to increase offerings. It must rather be a result of our being "fervent in our thinking" about our mission to America and the world. What is to be our response as we stand before the adventures of new frontiers in our lands? There must be a willingness to risk and a willingness to try. How fervent is our appeal to those who are going to a Christless grave? We often sit in our positions of comfort and security and whisper our message of hope and then we act surprised that no passerby is shaken from his lethargy and lostness. Lacking fervency, we are seemingly powerless to generate the energy that grasps and changes lives. From the safe refuge of padded pews and stained-glass windows we shout the gospel at the agony of alienation that is the world, wondering all the while why they don't come and join our holy band and on to glory go.

Fervency on mission will get us involved with the alienation that is our cities. Fervency on mission will get us involved with the human problems of crime, poverty, unemployment, and health care. Fervency on mission will get us involved in sharing our faith in Jesus Christ with those who have never heard and do not want to hear. This land cannot be evangelized and congregationalized by Christians infected with a spectator mentality. Fervency on mission will help us to take the dare of world evangelization. We will leave the known for the unknown, the tried for the untried, the humdrum for the adventure. The Bishop of Norway in his famous sermon during the Nazi occupation of Norway in a ringing militant call challenged the people of Norway to resistance and even death. During that message he said, "There is a foe. There is a fight. There is a faith." There is a foe whose "craft and power are great." There is a fight which will require "the whole armor of God." There is a faith that was "once delivered to the saints."

Roy McClain tells the story of an old blind man in China who was a convert of The China Inland Mission.[4] The old man had been blind for fifty years. At the mission the doctors looked at his eyes and discovered that he had cataracts that could be removed by surgery. They operated on him, and he regained almost all of his eyesight. For the first time in fifty years he could see. He was now, as a new believer, able to see both physically and spiritually. There was no happier person at the mission than the old man. Then one day he was gone. The missionaries wondered about the old man because he had not even told them good-bye and had made no expression of gratitude. He just vanished, and the missionaries had almost forgotten him when months later he came back. He was not alone. Over his shoulder was strung a rope almost 100 feet long and behind him hanging on the rope were almost fifty blind old men. He had gone back to his home village and then started back with his rope picking up blind men all along the way. He had been their eyes and their guide. He brought them back to the place where he had found sight.

It is time now to reach out to our nation. It is time for all of us who see to tell those who are blind where to find their sight. Evangelism is one who was once blind telling those who are blind where they can receive their sight. We cannot wait. Urgently they cry out in their blindness. Fervently we must go. Hear him saying to us, "We must work the works of Him who sent me while it is day, for the night is coming when no man can work." God help us to hurry before sundown.

Notes

1. David Redding, *The Parables He Told* (New York: Harper and Row, 1976), p. 5.
2. Carlyle Marney, *These Things Remain* (New York: Abingdon-Cokesbury, 1953), pp. 102-103.
3. Roy O. McClain, *This Way, Please* (Old Tappan: Fleming H. Revell Company, 1957), p. 179.
4. Ibid., p. 133.

2
My Church Is Missionary

The little old lady in the group touring Westminster Abbey was by no stretch of one's imagination the typical American tourist. She carried no camera. The little hat she wore was shapeless. Her rumpled dress looked like it might have been cut out of a wallpaper pattern. After a few exchanges of conversation with her, anyone would have been able to round out her story: a Bible-Belt grandmother who had always longed for a trip abroad and now her children were staking her to it. She had crowded into a few days her impossible itinerary. Watching her bounce from one spot of interest to another made one think that she had springs in her heels.

The tour guide had certainly met all the types by this time but he could not seem to tune in to this grandmother. She kept leading him instead of being led. She listened to every word of the droning descriptions, but her darting eyes and restlessness gave the tour guide the impression that she still had seen nothing that really impressed her. When she finally spoke, she broke into his pattern of thought with a question that left the tour guide slack jawed, puzzled, and humiliated. She asked, "Young man, tell me this (and she swept the panorama of the historic Abbey with a wrinkled hand), has anyone been saved here lately?"

As troublesome as that question appeared to be, as crudely put as it was, as impudent as it seems under the circumstances, it is a valid question for any Christian meetinghouse including the Abbey. When we get over the seeming inappropriateness of the grandmother's question, we really would like to have been there and said, "Grandmother, I don't know about the Abbey but

29

someone was saved in the services of our church last Sunday morning." We have a right to ask that question about my church and your church. When we look at the world in which we live and see the alienation from God, the frustration that afflicts our nation, and people dying from loneliness in the midst of a crowd, the question of the little old grandmother seems all the more relevant, "Has anyone been saved here lately?"

When you place the urgency of that question against the backdrop of the right now; when the voice of the cynic is heard throughout the land, insisting persuasively that it is almost closing time for our civilization; when people divide their time between silly amusements and slippery morality; when a dying civilization with the attitude of the late H. G. Wells says, "Don't bother me, can't you see I am busy dying at the moment?"—Isn't it about time we ask ourselves about our church, "Has anyone been saved here lately?" It may even be time for us to dust off some of those troublesome old words like "lost," "sin," "forgiven," "born again," and "condemned." In light of the world in which we are now living, they may not seem to be outmoded after all. The rumors of total oblivion that filter through the armed never-never land of our world seem to give this question a terrifying urgency.[1]

The question we are really asking is, "Is my church a missionary-evangelistic church?" Can we say, "My church is missionary"? In order to separate ourselves from those who are drunk on the sovereignty of God, we nail up signs telling the world that we are a "Missionary Baptist Church." But does that really make us missionary? There are churches that are "near-sighted." They see everything in terms of what's up front and close. They have great programs to reach the community through the media. They spend all of their resources on themselves. There are other churches that are "far-sighted." They are involved in supporting world missions sacrificially. However, they are not involved in witnessing to their neighbors. Their baptistries, except for rare occasions, stay bone dry. The church that sees things clearly sees missions and evangelism as alternate heartbeats of the church. The missionary church is the church whose survival goals do not eclipse its goals to live by dying and get by giving.

Can a church be a missionary church whose membership is cluttered up with well-meaning but spiritually anemic people who have never taken Christ seriously? Can a church be a missionary church whose members have gone through years of developing a thick armor plate of indifference so that the most scathing and searching accusations of Christ neither challenge them nor touch them? "Christ never meant for the church to be the ticket window to eternity."[2] He meant for it to be a power in the present community, nation, and world. He never meant for it to be a congregation of the respectable who saunter in and out of the precincts of God on Sunday mornings. He meant for it to be the body of Christ on mission in his world. Christ did not intend for the church to be a decoration for society when he spoke it into existence. He meant for the church to be salt, leaven, and light in society, loving, changing, redeeming. The church is not a mutual admiration society that meets only for the members to say nice things about one another. The church is a band of spiritual freedom fighters, committed to his cause and to exposing and eliminating shirking, hypocrisy, and betrayal in their own ranks.

Persons and nations reach a flood tide in their own lives. The flood tide is that moment in our lives or the life of a nation when what we do determines the whole direction of our lives as persons or as a nation. Jesus Christ had come to such a moment at Caesarea-Philippi. What he had been attempting to teach his disciples about himself finally had been stated. Peter, who had often in the past said the wrong thing, now says (and God love him for it) the right thing. "You are the Christ, the Son of the living God." When he was sure that those who followed him knew who he was, he could build what was his only legacy—a church. What he says to Peter, the other disciples, and to us after that is basic to our understanding of our theme for this chapter, "My Church Is Missionary."

And Jesus answered and said to him, "Blessed are you, Simon Barjona, because flesh and blood did not reveal this to you, but My Father who is in heaven. And I also say to you that you are Peter, and upon this rock I will build

My church; and the gates of Hades shall not overpower it. I will give you the keys of the kingdom of heaven; and whatever you shall bind on earth shall have been bound in heaven, and whatever you shall loose on earth shall have been loosed in heaven (Matt. 16:17-19).

The picture of the church he speaks into existence is not a picture of a timid church cowering behind stained-glass windows afraid of the world, the devil, and the future. The picture is a church battering at the very gates of death, rescuing the perishing, loosing and binding on earth what will be bound and loosed in eternity. This is not a picture of a lot of little mousy people constantly apologizing for what they believe. Our faith is no faith at all if it must be isolated, sheltered, and saved. Our faith is no faith at all if it cannot stand the wear and tear of everyday life. It is anemic and powerless if it cannot stand against the deepest questions of human thought and existence without cowering. We must discover a faith with four faces—the face of a lion, the face of an eagle, the face of a cherub, and the face of a human being. We need the face of a lion for courage, the face of an eagle for vision, the face of a cherub for innocence, and the face of a human for intelligence. It will take all of that to be good stewards of the binding and loosing.

How will we reproduce such a church with such a missionary-evangelistic compulsion that we can say, "My church is missionary"? How is it possible to enlist persons in the mission of the church when for them even church attendance and support no longer represent a religious obligation? Most of these people would be called "good" people. They do not want to live in a community without a "good" church. In the midst of a world in crisis can an ordinary church make any kind of significant contribution to evangelizing the community and the world? Our answer must be in the Scriptures. What was it that turned these first-century Christians into functioning missionary evangelists? Isn't the answer in the passage that we quoted from Matthew's Gospel? The disciples were discipled until they were crystal clear as to who Jesus Christ is and then they were sent out to evangelize the world. Are we really clear about our Leader? Do we know that he is Lord? Do we know that his last command was to go into the whole creation and preach the gospel to every human being on this planet?

My church is missionary because. . . . If you had to finish that sentence in 50 words or less, what would you say? You might give us the amounts of money your church gave to missions last year. You might give us the number of persons your church baptized last year. You might tell us that your church initiated a ministry in a deprived neighborhood. You might tell us that your church made a trip to another city and helped a group of people erect a building. You might tell us that you sent your pastor on an evangelistic mission in a foreign country. These are the results of some missionary zeal on the part of some persons in the church. They are the results and not reasons.

The reasons are basic. How we get our missionary-evangelism task done is important but it is not most important. The most important factors are the fundamentals. They are the basic reasons for our being missionary. The most important factor in our failure to become the missionary-evangelistic church our Lord intends for us to be is our failure to grasp these fundamentals. Our failures are theological. They are visionary failures. The reason our Lord spent so much of his time demonstrating and illustrating who he was is that this understanding is basic to mission. Solid work is impossible without solid doctrine. The task is impossible without the teaching. We do not lose what is important in the Christian faith until we lose what is most important. You do not lose the Lord's Day until you lose the resurrection. You do not lose lay ministry until you lose the priesthood of believers. You do not lose Christian living until you lose the new birth. You do not lose evangelism until you lose the atonement. What we believe determines what we do.

The Founder of the Church Is a Missionary

My church is missionary because our founder is a missionary. The thought about not losing some factor in Christian practice until you lose some factor in Christian faith can be carried two steps beyond the previous paragraph. You don't lose Christian missions until you lose the Great Commission. You don't lose the Christian church until you lose Jesus Christ. The sobering fact is that you can give mental assent to everything orthodox Christianity says about Christ and not really know him personally as Lord and Savior. The church can lose Christ and cease to be his church while still loudly proclaiming faith in him. Our failures are not failures to give assent to a creed about him, but failures in not being like him in personal life and commitment. The very word *Christian* means Christlike. There are many ways in which we are to be like he is, but one of those ways is pivotal for the discussion in this chapter.

Our Lord is a missionary. The very thought of the incarnation in the heart of God before the world began is a missionary thought. He came as a volunteer on mission to God's world. The writer of Hebrews must have had this thought in mind when he writes: "Then I said, 'Behold, I have come (In the roll of the book it is written of Me) to do Thy will, O God' " (Heb. 10:7). The writer of Hebrews used Psalm 40 for this great missionary text. This is the song of the voluntary servant on the mission of his master. A star was sent on a missionary journey across the heavens to proclaim his birth. When his ministry began in the synagogue at Nazareth, he chose a great missionary text from Isaiah. The urgency of his missionary task throbs on the pages of all four Gospels. If the church is the church at all, it must follow him on mission.

He has promised us that he will build the church. It is a promise that is ratified by resurrection. Our task is to bear the message on mission. We are to announce that he has come and that he is Lord and Savior. The Holy Spirit will use that announcement to bring to conviction and conversion those who believe. If we take care of the message on mission, he will build his church. That must be the naked, childlike, unadorned faith of the church. The church does not need better press, it needs better people. The church does not need more money, it needs more mission. The church does not need more agencies, it needs

more action. The church by holy living, holy growing, holy giving, and holy going lifts up Jesus Christ as the sinner's only hope,
humanity's only help, and a lost race's only haven. He has promised, "And I, if I be lifted up from the earth, will draw all men to
Myself" (John 12:32). The One who spoke these words was
about to die. He would be lifted up on a cross and die in expia-
tion of the world's sin. It was what he came to do. It was his mission. He says to the church for which he died, "Peace be with
you; as the Father has sent Me, I also send you" (John 20:21).

In the last hours of his life the missionary Lord was condemned by a coward, betrayed by a hypocrite, and denied by a
disciple. The fickle crowd that had cried, "Hosanna to the King,"
on Sunday cried, "Crucify him," on Friday. Before we get too
eager to condemn the betrayers and hypocrites who lived long
ago and far away, perhaps we need to take a good long look at
ourselves up close and up front. Have we betrayed him by failing
his mission? By disobedience to his final dying command to go
into all the world and make disciples and gather disciples into
missionary churches, have we discounted the very reason for
which he was born and for which he died? It is not a body of
teaching or a system of philosophy that enrobes the New Testament church with the power of the keys, the power to bind and
loose. A Person gives the church that power. The degree to
which the church incarnates the missionary Jesus Christ, to that
degree it has the power of the keys.

Among my souvenirs in a dresser drawer is my treasure chest
in which I have some things that I consider very valuable and
precious. One thing is a faded, yellowed-with-age photograph. It
is dog-eared from much handling. If I offered to sell it to you, you
would smile and politely refuse to buy it. There is something else
there. There is an old, worn out Lady Elgin watch that quit running years ago. It is a brooch that was pinned to clothing long
since lost in time. You would not want to buy the watch either. It
would be worthless to you. You could not buy them from me at
any price. Why do I value those old relics from another day so
much? Because they are all that I have that is tangible of the

second finest woman I have ever known. She carried that photograph in her purse for thirty years and wore that brooch watch pinned to her dress longer than that. They are a part of a precious legacy passed on to me from that wonderful woman, my mother.

Need you ask now why I think that the church, its mission and his commission are so precious to me and to all believers? It is everything he left us. He did not found a school for us to support. He left no institutions that bear his mission. He left us a church, a mission, and a commission. He called it "my" church. Paul, the master church planter, said that "Christ also loved the church and gave Himself up for her" (Eph. 5:25). The only reason I can call it "my" church is that first of all it is "His" church. The church is his body and is the continuing incarnation of him in the world. It is his church when it resembles him. It is only his church to the degree that it is created in his likeness. He came as a missionary on a mission and his church is a missionary church on his mission in his world. This statement cannot be made too much of or repeated too often. It is a fundamental concept of the Christian faith.

The church that he is building is a church on mission. That sense of mission is both personal for individual members of the church body and for the body life of the church. How many of the members of our churches have a sense of being on mission? With most of them isn't it really a matter of "coming to church" rather than "being on mission"? It is a beautiful fall Sunday morning in the Southern United States and the First Baptist Church is about to make the shattering announcement that Jesus Christ is alive and that he is Lord. There will be persons there that will be faced with life or death, heaven or hell. What is the topic of animated conversation just before the service of worship and gospel proclamation? Are they talking about the persons who are there who need Christ? Are they bowed in prayer for a visitation of the power of God? Are they talking in small groups about the old drunk that died without Christ in a doorway last night? Are they whispering prayers for the prodigal girl that lives just down the street? No, they are talking about almighty football. That was also the topic of conversation at the local pub on Saturday night. Out of the 100 or 500 members of your church, how many would you say have a sense of mission?

Men and women in the armed forces know what a commission is. Do churches know what a commission ratified by resurrection is? Do we really know that the words "commission" and "committed" and "mission" are interrelated? The mission is our task. The commission is the authority given to believers and to the church to engage in mission. Commitment is the quality of obedience and radical love that we make in response to his commission. Do you take seriously the commission? That can be answered with another question: What is the quality of your commitment? Many are only Christian "commuters" who drive into the religious downtown once a week to satisfy religious and cultural longings, but have never really bought into the mission. The bloody Man with five bleeding wounds is the only measure of the quality of our commitment that we have. My church is a missionary church because the founder of my church is a missionary.

The Foundation of My Church Is Missionary

My church is missionary because the foundation of my church is missionary. We used to sing, "How firm a foundation, ye saints of the Lord, is laid by your faith in his excellent Word!" His word is "Upon this rock I will build my church." The "rock" upon which he builds the church is not Peter nor even himself because the rock is neuter gender in the text. It could not have referred to any person. The text makes it clear that he is referring to the confession of Peter. That is the "rock" upon which the church is founded and built. It is the foundation rock of the confessional church. We return to our basic question, "Who is Jesus Christ?" When Peter answered, "You are the Christ, the Son of the Living God," it is the first time in the New Testament that anyone confesses him in this way. When the disciples have been discipled to the point that they have the right answer to this basic question, he speaks the church into existence. That confession makes disciples and the church is built. That confession spoken, whispered, transmitted, communicated, written, sung, and dramatized confronts persons with the question that faced Pontius Pilate, "What then shall I do with Jesus who is called Christ?" (Matt. 27:22). When that confession is made as an open statement of the truth, men are once again confronted with Jesus of Nazareth. It is a missionary statement. Its purpose is to lead men to God through Jesus Christ.

Is our lack of a sense of mission and a crusading spirit due to a lack of real conviction about who he is and what he demands of us? Peanuts really may have diagnosed our problem. Charlie Brown and Linus are discussing the issues in our world, and Linus remarks that when he grows up he wants to be a real fanatic. Charlie questions Linus as to what he wants to be a real fanatic about. With a toss of his head Linus replies, "Oh, I don't know. It doesn't really matter. I'll be a sort of wishy-washy fanatic." Isn't that exactly what we have too much of in the church? We should be rocklike in our conviction that Jesus Christ is the Son of God and Son of Man risen from the dead and living at the right hand of God where he intercedes for us. We have said words about him that have grown slick with repetition and bounce off the memory banks of our minds. It really never dawns on us that those words, "Jesus Christ is Lord," have meanings that demand radical responses from us.

Do we really believe that he is Lord? Do we really believe that the mission is important enough for even the Son of God to die for? Do we really believe that the millions who have never become Christians in this country will die and go to hell? Do we really believe that the gospel of Jesus Christ can save persons from a hell in eternity and a hell on earth? Isn't that our faith that we are constantly confessing from our pulpits, in our Sunday School lessons, and hopefully in our witnessing in the marketplace? But are we acting as though that is our faith? When was the last time we really made a sacrifice for his mission? When was the last time you or someone in your church shed a tear of concern for the non-Christians in your community? How many persons in your church are sharing their faith with some degree of regularity with persons who are not Christians? How much of your church's wealth went to meet the local church's needs and how much was shared with the world mission of the church? Have you ever spent one sleepless night in prayer for a lost world? Do you know of anyone who has? The confession that we make with our lips must not be betrayed by our actions and attitudes.

The church has the power of the keys. Faith and its confession are the keys of the kingdom of God. It is interesting that it is the "keys of" and not the "keys to" the kingdom of God. The very nature of the kingdom is the faith and its confession by believers. The historical arguments that have raged over the nature of the keys as to whether they are *Clavis Pontentiae*, the key of ecclesiastical power, or *Clavis Scientiae*, the key of ecclesiastical knowledge, may only be an exercise in futility. Alford, Wordsworth, Luther, Calvin, and many others say rightly that the keys were given to Peter and to all who confess the faith. A key is something that is precise and opens to someone who has it whatever it is that lies behind the closed door or in the treasured box. The confession of Peter is precise. Adoration, faith, and personal conviction are mingled together in this confession. "You are the Christ, the Son of the living God."

The missionary church is the church whose members cannot be silent. They must confess their faith. The confession of Peter is intellectually positive. It is emotionally frank. It is unashamedly open. The key is the key to mission. It is the foundation upon which the church is built. Peter did not say, "You are a great leader," or "You are a great prophet and teacher," or "You are a son of God," or "You are the perfect Nazarene," or "You are a divine person." The missionary church is the church that makes the confession that Peter made in an open statement of the truth to the non-Christian. The church does not stutter about "Who is Jesus Christ?" In this confession the uniqueness of the Christian faith is clearly stated. We have a great deal in common with Islam and with Judaism by way of heritage and teaching. But in this confession the lines are clearly drawn. This confession makes it clear that we cannot be a "wishy-washy fanatic" about him. There is no room for the objection, "Well, after all, they have their religion and we have ours. I think we ought to leave them alone. Live and let live, I always say."

The missionary thrust of the church is not threatened nearly so much by open universalism as it is by the unconscious universalism that often afflicts many church members and results in frivolous and foolish objections such as the one stated in the paragraph above. Most pastors agree that it is much easier to motivate persons to give large sums of money than it is to involve them in verbal witness. Jesus Christ is the Messiah. There is no other Savior. It is that conviction that has motivated all of the great missionaries of the church. It is that conviction that spurred the church to send missionaries to the next village, the next country, and to the ends of the earth. It is that conviction that made loud and insistent truth tellers of the first Christians witnessing to the great crowds in Jerusalem who came for the feast of Pentecost. The very foundation upon which the church stands and upon which it is built is the clear convincing confession that Jesus is the Christ, the Son of the Living God.

Peter was not without his fears. Why are we so afraid of verbal witnessing? Can we even dream of sharing our faith with the world when we cannot overcome our fears of the man next door? How can we expect laypersons to become fearless witnesses when many pastors frankly confess that they are afraid of personal witnessing? Why are we afraid of doing what seemed to be natural in the Christians of the first century? Is it that we don't know how? I am not sure that that is really the reason. I think that we may not be overwhelmed by who Jesus Christ is. We can continue to kid ourselves by saying, "That's just not my gift," but the truth may well be that we have never really seen up close and up front the breathtaking, heart-stopping, world-shattering miracle of the unthinkable, "You are the Christ, the Son of the Living God."

The Future of the Church Is Missionary

"And the gates of Hades shall not overpower it." The missionary faith is the faith of his resurrection and ours. One of the reasons that the disciples stayed in Jerusalem may have been their confidence in the second coming of Christ. Immediately after the resurrection, the early church had its back to the world and was facing the coming of the Lord. Its course was charted not by its task but by the star of its hope. The Book of Acts is the story of how God turned the church around to face the world. God used persecution to drive the church into the world (Acts 8:1 ff.). The church that fixes its eyes only upon Christ's return has a tendency to become introverted and segregated from the world. The message is, "Why stand there gazing . . . you shall be my witnesses to Jerusalem, Judea, Samaria, and the uttermost parts of the earth" (see Acts 1:8,11). The point is that the church must see the second coming as a motive to missionary zeal rather than something that the church is to spend her time looking for.

The compulsions that drive the church to its goal of world evangelization are two in number, one is geographical and the other eschatological. One is to go to the ends of the earth and the other is to go to the end of time. The church is looking for that day when we with John the revelator see that "great multitude, which no one could count, from every nation and all tribes and peoples and tongues, standing before the throne and before the Lamb, clothed in white robes, and palm branches were in their hands; and they cry out with a loud voice, saying 'Salvation to our God who sits on the throne, and to the Lamb' " (Rev. 7:9-10). But until then we have a task to do. The church is not to use the second coming to attempt to scare the world into repenting nor as an excuse to relax and wait. The second coming is a primary motivation to make my church and your church missionary churches which are restless as long as there is one person who has not heard.

This resurrection-missionary hope that, "the gates of Hades will not prevail against it," should incite us to the completion of our task. Remember that before he comes, the gospel is to be preached to all the peoples. A good modern translation of the Greek word translated "nations" is "ethnics." The Greek word even sounds like the English word. It is *ethne*. There is no better locus for the ethnic dimensions of our task than America. The Home Mission Board is responsible for every ethnic group in the world. Even ancient ethnic designations such as Afghans, Persians, and Babylonians are found in America in surprising numbers. Our mission to America is a mission to the world. No missionary agency in the world has the responsibility for reaching any more ethnic peoples than does the Home Mission Board. Jerusalem, Judea, and Samaria are all here. Many of these peoples have never been evangelized. Ethnic churches generally grow fast and become self-supporting soon after they are planted. In that great multitude that no man can number on that great day of resurrection will be many out of every tribe, tongue, and nation who were evangelized in America. There will be many there who were evangelized in some other nation by Christian relatives in the United States. While all history is rushing to his goal, we must work his works for the night is coming when no one will be able to work.

A very practical application is made in regard to the second coming at the point of our stewardship. This has a direct application, indeed, a critical application, at the point of our missionary task. Some of the great parables of Jesus relate stewardship and the second coming. Those parables would quite certainly include the parable of the talents, the parable of the pounds, the parable of the virgins, and the parable of the rich man and Lazarus. The world is in great need of the things that only money can provide and cannot be provided without money. Sick persons in inner cities need physicians that only money can provide. The ignorant, the handicapped, the retarded, and the poor need ministries that only money can provide. There are some practical questions that arise out of a serious consideration of the Lord's return as Peter suggests, "But the day of the Lord will come like a thief, in which the heavens will pass away with a roar and the elements will be destroyed with intense heat, and the earth and its works will be burned up. Since all these things are to be destroyed in this way" (2 Pet. 3:10-11*a*).

How much will a nice piece of property at the interstate interchange in Atlanta sell for one day after the Lord's return? How much interest will those certificates of deposit pay one day after he comes? What will be the value of that single-family dwelling then? What great conglomerate's stocks will do well on that day's market? Peter says, "Seeing that all these things will be destroyed." Seeing that is so, to what use should we put our possessions now? It may have been a lot easier for the early church to give everything they had since they really believed he might be coming the next day and all of it would be worth nothing. How long has it been since the members of your church gave diamond rings, money saved up for new drapes or a summer vacation, shares of stock or deeds to property to feed the hungry, heal the sick, build churches, and minister to the helpless and hopeless? Which ones of us on that day of reckoning will hear, "I was hungry and you fed me, I was thirsty and you gave me drink, I was naked and you clothed me, I was in prison and you visited me?" Dare we take those words from final judgment seriously? It is not right to say that we must focus our attention on things eternal and not on money for it is temporal. Money is not temporal for it goes into the shaping of life and destiny. All things are spiritual when handled by spiritual persons and put to spiritual use.

Involvement with the church means involvement with something eternal. To know Jesus Christ as Lord and Savior is to have eternal life. The Hebrew text of Ecclesiastes 3:11 says that God has put eternity in our hearts. The pessimistic Koheleth of the Old Testament and the church planter of the New Testament do not have much else in common, but Paul says, "Set your affection on things that are above." Christ in his teaching and Paul in his epistles laid great stress on the eternal consequences involved in this life and in the missionary activity of the church. The people of God are the people who have believed the incredible, seen the invisible, and attempted the impossible. The church needs a vision of the eternal. The future of the church in the kingdom of God puts the church and its missionary task in a new perspective for us. We are not engaged in something that will be destroyed—not even by atomic holocaust. The bomb can destroy everything that is visible, but the invisible is untouchable.

"My church is missionary because the founder of my church is a missionary, the foundation of my church, its faith, and confession are missionary, and because the future of my church is a missionary future when persons from every tribe, tongue, and nation will go into the Kingdom." That's my statement on "My church is missionary because. . . ." The answer is a winner, because he is a winner. The antiphonal choirs in Revelation 5 sing "the new song" about the winner.

The twenty-four elders sing:

Worthy art Thou to take the book, and to break its seals; for Thou wast slain, and didst purchase for God with Thy blood men from every tribe and tongue and people and nation. And Thou hast made them to be a kingdom and priests to our God; and they will reign upon the earth (vv. 9-10).

The angels and the living creatures sing:

Worthy is the Lamb that was slain to receive power and riches and wisdom and might and honor and glory and blessing (v. 12).

Then all created things join in:

To Him who sits on the throne, and to the Lamb, be blessing and honor and glory and dominion forever and ever (v. 13).

The four living creatures were all the while saying: "Amen."

Notes

1. Frederick B. Speakman, *The Salty Tang* (Westwood: Fleming H. Revell Company, 1954), pp. 11-14.
2. Carlyle Marney, *These Things Remain* (New York: Abingdon-Cokesbury, 1953), pp. 102-103.

3

The Einstein Factor

On a spring day in 1921 aboard the boat deck of the steamship *Rotterdam*, a little man in a dingy gray raincoat and a floppy black hat faced a battery of newspaper reporters. Faded gray hair that was later to become the object of ridicule straggled out of the floppy hat around his ears and over the collar of the dingy gray coat. The next morning the *New York Times* carried stories on the front page, "Talk in Ireland of Peace and War," "Harding Summons Rail Men's Leaders," "Illinois Legion Protests Against Release of Debts," and one that seems peculiarly up-to-date, "Two Strangely Shot in Madison Square Park." What the little man had to say was buried on page five of the *Times*. "Einstein sees the end of time and space. Destruction of the material universe would be followed by nothing says the creator of relativity. He says his theory is logically simple."

The Harding administration was only weeks old, and the new president seemed to confess the attitude of the country toward the new theories when he admitted that he was confused by them. John Sharp Williams, senator from Mississippi famous for his eloquent tongue and his silver moustache, said for *The Congressional Record*, "I frankly confess that I do not understand Einstein; I frankly confess that I do not believe that the senator from Pennsylvania understands Einstein—and I do not believe that even the senator from Massachusetts [Henry Cabot Lodge with a PhD from Harvard] would make a positive pretense in that direction."

Einstein was not only difficult to understand but also controversial. One newspaper editorial complained about his unkempt

45

hair and whiskers. A *Times* editorial said, "The Declaration of Independence itself is outraged by the assertion that there is anything on earth or in interstellar space that can be understood only by a chosen few." The attacks came from both anti-intellectual and anti-Semitic groups in the United States. Here on a visit to raise funds for the yet unborn state of Israel, Einstein found himself a controversial figure on a controversial mission. After he received the Nobel Prize in 1922, the Communist Party of the Soviet Union in a special meeting condemned his theories as "the product of the bourgeois class in decomposition." After his return to Germany he was finally forced to flee as an exile back to the United States.

There were still doubters even after the experiments with the planet Mercury proved him right. When his famous formula $E = MC^2$ gave us the mushroom cloud over Hiroshima and Nagasaki there were more believers.

Einstein gave us a new universe. His revolutionary physics along with the work of Max Planck and Niels Bohr made the world of Newtonian physics obsolete. Man, influenced by the classical Newtonian physics, stood on the edge of a fully understandable, self-corrective universe governed by unchanging laws. There he proclaimed his own genius with no need for God. We now stand in the fourth dimensional space-time continuum looking into the eternity of a black hole with the eerie electronic music of distant quarks playing hymns of mysteries beyond our understanding. Suddenly old-fashioned words like "resurrection" and "redeemed" and "mystery" have new meanings.

The God who was banished from heaven by Karl Marx, imprisoned in the subconscious by Sigmund Freud, erased from nature by Charles Darwin, and declared definitely dead by Friedrich Nietzsche is today making a strong comeback. It is very respectable now to talk about God in the world of science and philosophy where only decades ago God was consigned to the basement with broken tools and worn-out toys. *Time* magazine in the April 7, 1980, issue reviews the resurrection of the old arguments for God now respected by some of the greatest minds. One theologian has said, "The experiment with secularism finally proved too much for the human psyche to cope with, both in the Marxist world and our world." The Society for Christian Philosophy now numbers 300.

Two millenniums ago another Jew who was also misunderstood and also very controversial came preaching and teaching. When he left this world the victim of crucifixion, he left his church to live in his continuum of time and space. His only legacy to the world was a band of witnesses, a church. His order to the church was to go to the ends of the earth until the end of time. "You shall be My witnesses both in Jerusalem, and in all Judea and Samaria, and even to the remotest ends of the earth . . . why do you stand looking into the sky? This Jesus, who has been taken up from you into heaven, will come in just the same way as you have watched Him go into heaven" (Acts 1:8,11). He left the church a memorial supper before which we stand to swear loyalty to him in a festal supper that "proclaims the Lord's death until he comes." We are not to stand gazing but to "occupy until he comes."

Paul, under the missionary compulsion of time and space, tells the Corinthians that it is a time of emergency for the church. All the frills of life are to be laid aside for the urgencies of the mission. He says, "Brothers, the time is short" (1 Cor. 7:29). If the Einstein factor changed the shape of the universe and made room for God, the Jesus factor changed the shape of our existence as believers and leaves room for nothing except the missionary imperative to go to the ends of the earth until the end of time.[1]

The Missionary Christ stands on the resurrection side of his grave and says to all who love and follow him, "The world in which you have lived is dead; you now live in a new world. It is a world in which nothing has meaning except in relation to my mission which is your mission. Your world is no longer Jewish or Gentile. You who have been 'no people' are now 'the people of God.' I have given you a mission, a message, and a mandate. Go to the ends of the earth and make disciples until I come. Go to the ends of the earth for every man deserves to hear in his own tongue the good news of deliverance. Go to the end of time for men who are born, live, and die, and every new generation is a new world that must be evangelized."

He says to us, "Go to the cities of your own land. Some of those cities have more Jews than Jerusalem, more Poles than Warsaw, more Czechs than Prague. Go to the cities of your country where the action is: the neon and the noise, the paychecks and the poverty, the experimentation and the exploitation, the museums and the murders, the loneliness and the lovelessness, the glory and the grime, the shattered dreams and the sleepless nights. Go to the cities where dreams are born and lives are ruined; where violence cries out for peace, where poverty weeps for relief; where anonymity reaches out for friends." Shrugging off all his urging, we run from the city rather than go to it. We are afraid of the city. Its stone and steel shoulders are cold and unyielding. Its acrid smoky breath chokes us. Its garish lights, dark doorways, and shadowy figures threaten us. We need a new birth of compassion to help us see through his eyes the disillusioned, the disinherited, the disenfranchised, and the disowned in the ghettos of loneliness and rejection.

He says to us, "Go and learn from me on my mission." Proclaim in imitation of me as I came preaching the gospel of the Kingdom. Learn how to be truth tellers to counter all the evil one's lies. In argument, in proclamation, in teaching, in discussing, in gossiping press my claims as Lord upon all. Press my claims until I become the topic of discussion in the universities and the supermarkets, in the classrooms and laundromats, on the planes and in the subways. Witness in your marketplace. Make the traffic pattern of your life your pulpit. By life and by lip give credible evidence to my transforming power. In imitation of me know that you have been born again to minister and to die. Know that the price of ministry is the death of self. You must do more than learn from me, you must learn me. You must be an incarnation of me. If I am to live at all in the lives of the lost I must live first in you."

Have you felt the impact of the missionary Christ who calls us as Lord to be on mission to the ends of the earth until the end of time? Can you honestly believe that our pastors, our churches, and our denominational leaders are now being compelled by that personal, pressing, and passionate necessity to evangelize this nation? It is a fact of the Scriptures and of experience that our commitment to missions and our witnessing stand or fall together. Believing that "God so loved the world," that in Christ he gave everything he had, means that the one who uses those words is committed to make witnessing the controlling principle of life. That is the essence of missions.

Evangelism as the concern for bringing our country to Christ is not something that we can pick and choose from as in a cafeteria serving line. It is not something optional like the multicolored coupons on the back page of the Sunday supplement in the *Atlanta Journal-Constitution*. It is rather something that is rooted indefeasibly in the character of God who has come to us in Jesus Christ. Evangelism and missions are not the province of a few enthusiasts in the church but the raison d'etre for the church's existence. They are not something for a few ecclesiastical specialists, but they are every Christian's job. Sharing the gospel is the distinctive mark of being a Christian, and the desire to take the good news to the ends of the earth is the birthmark of the believer. Accepting Christ as Savior and Lord is enlistment under a missionary banner.

The Urgency of His Claim

He stands on the mountain of his ascension, the missionary Christ, as *Christus Victor*, victorious over death, hell, and the grave and says to us, "All authority has been given me. Go to the ends of the earth and the end of time." He makes this claim as Lord *(Kurios)*. Wielding the full office of his providence, claiming the full knowledge of his omniscience, exercising the full power of his omnipotence, he says to us, "Go as a missionary people and evangelize the earth until everyone has heard or until I come again." We cannot question his authority. We cannot quibble about his direction; we cannot quake before the daring adventure to which he calls us. He is Lord.

Our Commander in Chief who calls us to mission is perfect in his work of redemption, preeminent in his plan of salvation, powerful in his goal of reconciliation, and prominent in the merit of his mediation. He commands us to go, beginning in our backyard, to the ends of the earth. We are to evangelize our own neighborhood, our own county, our own suburbia, our own inner city and from there to every person on the earth. None must be forgotten; none must be overlooked; none must be neglected. He has the right to command. He is Lord. He has a right to command pastors and people, churches and associations, state conventions and agencies. He makes missions and evangelism the number one priority of churches and denominations. We have no power or right to reorder his priorities. To the ends of the earth until the end of time is the supreme preoccupation of his church, his people, his denomination until he comes.

Most significantly he has the right to command me. I live under the compulsion of his command. I have no right and you have no right to claim prior commitments, more urgent matters, or lesser objectives. Love and obedience leave us with no options. We must obey now. Procrastination is fatal to discipleship and the mission. The texts that are so often pressed upon the non-Christian beseeching immediate obedience are probably more aptly directed to believers. "I must first go home and bury my father" was a lame excuse for discipleship. Churches say, "When we get this building paid for, we will put a great emphasis on missions." Christians say, "When I get more time and my career demands are not so heavy, I will witness." The Commander says, "Go now." The mission is weighted with opportunity now.

If the president of the United States called us to a priority, I suspect that most citizens would consider it a mandate. Men who command us here have limitations, but the One who commands us as Lord is limitless. Those who exercise authority on earth are marked by boundaries of power and authority, but our Commander is omnipotent and without limits. He has the right to

command the priority of our missionary task for he alone fur-
nished the foundations of our faith. He alone is the biding author
of our eternal salvation. He alone is the One who satisfied infinite
justice with once-for-all atonement. He alone is the One who
justifies all who believe. He alone is the One who interceded at
the right hand of God as the guarantor of our salvation.

He has the ability to accomplish as well as the ability to enable.
He will not send us out to become failures. We cannot argue our
depleted treasuries, or the necessity of our luxuries, or the weakness of our ranks. These arguments simply will not compute
when we have already preprogrammed his ability. When we
argue our weakness, he stands and calls to us across the centuries, "My strength is made perfect in weakness" (2 Cor. 12:9,
KJV). When we argue our necessities, he reminds us that "the
Son of Man has nowhere to lay His head" (Matt. 8:20). When
we argue our lack of funds, he says to us again, "My Father
knows your needs. Ask what you will and it shall be done" (see
Matt. 6:8;7:7). Only out of the resources of his enabling can we
discover the graciousness to go, the generosity to give, and the
gratitude to respond to his call to our mission to America.

To enable us for the accomplishment of his mission he offers
us his enormous energies, his prodigious powers, and his abso-
lute authority. The quantities and qualities of this energy, power,
and authority pour the acid of his anger upon our indifference,
our hesitation, and our willingness to mark time while millions of
our fellow citizens die Christless deaths and go to Godless
graves. This urgency has a way of focusing on us when we
remember that our lives are limited by time. It is not difficult for
me to interpret this in a very personal way. The time will come, if
he does not come first, when I will no longer be able to preach
the good news. The night may come when men will no longer
hear—when doors now open will be closed to the message of
saving grace in Jesus Christ. Even that ultimate threat—the
nuclear cloud—black, impenetrable—hangs over our existence.
The ultimate night of man's self-destruction could end forever
our opportunity.

It is unbelievable that Christians who continually urge non-Christians to accept the urgent need for becoming a Christian, should act themselves as if they had forever to fulfill their mission and share their testimony with the whole world. Some churches continue to give buildings, community image, and survival goals priority over the mission. Christians continue to give pleasure, work, and self-enjoyment priority over the mission. Is it possible for our Lord to remain in the midst of a life, a church, an agency, or a denomination that forfeits its missionary character and calling? I do not believe he can. Is it possible for our Lord to be present in a group of believers who have shelved their responsibility for evangelism? I do not believe he will. The "lo" and "go" of the Great Commission are inseparably linked in his last promise. The condition for possessing Christ within the body is linked to our obedience to share without the body.

The Authority of His Command

The urgency of his claim waits on our submission to him as Lord. The authority of his command waits on our obedience to him as Leader. The nation for which our Lord has given us sacred responsibility faces many challenges today. We are being tried in the fiery furnace of serious divisions. There are social issues that threaten to tear us apart. On the international scene global brinkmanship has moved the very survival of life on our planet to "the front of the line." It is understandable that people are both frightened and confused. The technology which we hoped would bring us into a new age of life at its best has turned out to be the greatest threat to our existence that we have ever faced. There is a deep fear that man's new power to colonize the stars and to engineer genetics will be possessed by demonic powers.

The "unman" of C. S. Lewis is a possibility. Darth Vader becomes more and more flesh and blood rather than a creature of Hollywood's imagination. A furtive secret fear of global extinction lurks in the darkest depths of the collective consciousness. The final towering issue of the last twenty years of this millennium may well be the survival of humanity. We could end up becoming in humanity's last hours spiritual zombies rushing madly to the blind alleys and cul-de-sacs of the credit-card culture mumbling our litanies of death: "When you carry Master Charge, you carry clout," "You only go around once in life," and "Have it your way." The world is all dressed up with no place to go. When the hour of apocalypse comes, they will explode in a nuclear hell still clutching their plastic gods who promised them a "brave new world."

While millions in a sin-satiated, drug-debauched, and self-serving nation face economic disaster, mass suicide and nuclear hell are going no place because they have no place to go. The church having a place to go and a reason for going all too often sits behind its stained-glass barriers polishing its medals won by a previous and more heroic generation. The superficial church built on false values is algebraic rather than geometric. It draws up pretty patterns but ignores vital relationships. To that church outward form is more important than inward renewal, institutions are more important than people, and participation more important than consecrations. If we are not careful, enrollment becomes synonymous with salvation.[2]

Our Leader calls us from the superficial to the church where enthusiasm is the unfailing flag of the Holy Spirit. His church does not have opinions but convictions, and the heart of that conviction is mission and missions. His church does not confuse the voice of man for the voice of God. His church does not excuse shoddy workmanship under a gloss of pious intentions. It never gets fat on lip service while confusing commotion with motion, and clichés with truth. It never preempts the place of a valid center of value by denying the tragedy, suffering, and tension-ridden agonies of this present world. It never tries to escape the possibility of being confronted by a vital Christianity by taking bypasses of cultural adaptability. It never joins its culture in escaping Christ by a strategic retreat from the vital frontiers of spiritual need.

The church that will not follow its Leader finds the defense of the inner city too costly and resolves to hold onto the side streets of suburbia. Deafened by its self-praise and blinded by its own survival it takes its timid journey adapting, minimizing, external- izing, and idolizing. That church that has abandoned the narrow way and narrow gate of its Leader avoids by substitution, diver- sion, or denial the scandal of the cross and the sacrifice of self without which there is no real faith, no real Christianity. The Leaderless church finds its own leaders in persons it makes in its own image. Religious superstars and electronic ego maniacs replace church leaders made in the image of the One who "made of himself no reputation." Monies raised in the name of missions and evangelism may finance large estates, expensive automo- biles, and ornate temples.

What our Lord as Leader is saying to us in this command that we have chosen to call the Great Commission, we cannot avoid or evade. To avoid it is cowardice; to evade it is treason. Before his death he sent his disciples out to the lost sheep of the house of Israel. Now he is sending us to the ends of the earth until the end of time. He wants us to go to the inner cities of spiritual need where the unloved and unloving are haunted by the three horse- men of the ghetto: crime, drugs, and unemployment. He wants us to go to swank suburbs where alcoholism, drug addiction, and sexual license are hidden by a thin veneer of education, money, and social acceptability. He wants us to go to the thou- sands of unevangelized and unchurched where hundreds of thousands with no word from the beyond cry out of Christless need, "How can we hear without a preacher?" The missionary Christ as Lord and Leader of those of us who have dared to fol- low him calls all of us to mission.

The Reliability of His Compensation

He is Lord by the claim that he makes. He is Leader by the command that he issues. He is also Lover by the compensation that he offers the believer, the church, and the denomination that takes his missionary manifesto seriously. In Revelation 1:5 he is "the One loving us." He is the One among the seven golden candlesticks (the churches) as Lover. The Commission makes it clear that his presence with us is promised to the missionary pastor, the missionary church, and the missionary denomination. To have him is everything. Not to have him is to have nothing. He said pointedly that if we love him we will keep his commands. Can we really say and sing that we love him when we have been disloyal to our Lord, disobedient to our Leader, and disappointing to our Lover in not taking seriously his mission and our missionary obligation?

What is more important to a church or denomination than anything else? Isn't it the presence and power of Christ? His presence with us is not relative to our orthodoxy or our profession. It is related only to our unquestioned obedience to him. What is it that he offers us as compensation for our obedience? He offers us only his presence. If we want him, then we must obey him. We cannot ignore the Great Commission nor can we ignore the great commandment. Loving him with all of our strength, with all our minds, with all our souls means quite simply—obedience. The love of God in Jesus Christ requires only one response—radical love. That radical love issues in radical obedience. The missionary command is not his only command, but it is his last command before leaving earth. It is his priority command. If the Lover of our souls is to be with us, we must go with him on mission.

We can determine that we will have him above everything else in our own lives, in our churches, and in all of our denominational life. We can give his mission to the ends of the earth and to the end of time, his priority in our giving, in our living, in our calling out the called, and in enlisting volunteers. We can submit to him as Lord, obey him as Leader, and love him as Lover. He is the missionary Christ, and his mission is our mission. We are to complete what he began when he first came preaching the kingdom of God. What he did in calling out disciples and equipping them for mission we can now bring to completion.

Teaching as never man taught, he declared the Father's love and will as a missionary.

Seeking as never man sought, he found the lost and rescued them as a missionary.

Working as never man wrought, he went from place to place preaching as a missionary.

Buying as never man bought, he drank the bitter cup and died the awful death as a missionary.

Fighting as never man fought, he faces the powers of earth and hell and won as a missionary.

Bringing as never man brought, he presented to the Father all the trophies of grace as a missionary.

We can agree that we will follow him our missionary Christ as Lord, Leader, and Lover of his church. We are on his mission, traveling not by a schedule but by faith. Like Abraham we want to walk right off the map with him and go where they have never heard to the uncharted and unknown. That is the risk of faith. We will follow him to the ends of the earth and until time for us is no more. We will not go first and bury our father. We will not worry about pieces of land and blue-chip investments. Until we know that his omnipotence is overthrown, we will claim his power for mission. Until we hear that his almightiness has been abolished, we will undertake for him on mission. Until we hear that his immutability is imperiled, we will stand by him on mission. Until we read that his covenant with us is canceled, we will go with him on mission. Until we learn that his superiority is superseded, we will succeed with him on mission. Until we sense that his faithfulness is failing, we will depend on him on mission. Until we deem that his purposes are paralyzed, we will hope with him on mission. Until we discern that his kingdom is crumbling, we will evangelize with him on mission. Until his pledge is fulfilled in the kingdom of God and all the kingdoms of this world become the kingdom of our God and his Christ, we will follow him to the ends of the earth and the end of time.

Notes

1. Some of the ideas are from James W. Angell, *Put Your Arms Around the City* (Old Tappan: Fleming H. Revell Company, 1970).

2. Carlyle Marney, *Faith in Conflict* (New York: Abingdon Press, 1957), see pp. 104-107.

4
The Three Senses of Mission

Marie Antoinette lived in a world she refused to see, to hear, and to touch. Born into a world of frills and finery as the daughter of Emperor Francis I and Maria Theresa, she never actually saw the real world of pain and suffering, of poverty and alienation. She refused to look at the world around her. When she went to her wedding in Notre Dame, she ordered that all cripples and beggars be removed from the route of the royal carriage so she would not be able to see them. She did not want her marriage spoiled by the sight or sound of pain and sorrow. Her marriage to the Duc de Berri, Dauphin of France, was not to be marred by looking at suffering or calamity. Unconsciously she was taking the surest path to the destruction of her own happiness. The surest way to her own happiness would have been to have given special care and attention to the unfortunate ones of her kingdom.

If she had allowed the common people to line the route, and had stopped the carriage to see, hear, and touch the sights, sounds, and misery of the unfortunate, she would have been acclaimed "their queen." The wedding bells of Notre Dame would have then sung a much happier song. What she did not know was that her wedding processional was in reality a funeral march. The same persons that she refused to see, hear, and touch would send her to prison in August of 1793, and order her to the guillotine in October. Her faults were due to her narrow childhood, her imprisonment by luxury, her limited education, and her failure to see the world around her with sympathy and understanding.

57

One of the greatest passages in all the Scriptures is the third chapter of Exodus. It is great because it gives us a New Testament conception of God. Long before Jesus Christ was ever born, an incident takes place in the life of Israel that reveals the character of God as love. The Scriptures say, "And the Lord said, I have surely seen the affliction of my people which are in Egypt, and have heard their cry by reason of their taskmasters; for I know their sorrows; and I am come down to bring them . . . up out of that land unto a good land and a large" (Ex. 3:7-8, KJV). God is on mission in Exodus 3. God says that he has seen, he has heard, and now he comes down to touch the sorrow and the anguish of his people. Here in the second book of the Bible are the three senses of mission.

John, in his first epistle, applies the three senses to the very experience of salvation itself. He says, "That which was from the beginning, which we have heard, which we have seen with our eyes, which we have looked upon, and our hands have handled, of the Word of Life" (1 John 1:1, KJV). John appeals to these three basic senses as testimony to the reality of what he and others have experienced in Christ. There are many other passages in the Gospels that say, "Jesus saw," "Jesus heard," "Jesus touched."

What is it that makes a church blind, deaf, and unfeeling to the world God loves? Is it that the church is captured by a very affluent culture? Is it often due to the limited mission education of the average church member? Is it because of our refusal to open a heart of compassion to the world around us? Whatever the reason, the refusal to open our eyes to the plight of the poor and hungry, to unstop our ears to the cries of the victims of injustice, and to touch with Christ's love the lost and the sinful are fatal to missionary zeal. We may never be guillotined as was Marie Antoinette for our insensitivity, but can we escape the judgment of God?

Are we as Christians guilty of not only being blind but also wanting to be blind to the needs of the poor, deaf to the cries of the lonely, and numb to the pain of the hurting? Jesus calls all believers to a union with him to see the world as he sees it, hear the world as he hears it, and touch the world as he touches it.

When disciples enrolled in his school, his first lessons for them were lessons in compassion. He pointed to the epileptic writhing in the dust. "Look," he said, "look at the body shaken by convulsions. Look and care." He cupped his ear and said, "Listen, listen to the screams of anguish coming from that house where a young mother cuddles and rocks a dead baby. Listen and care." "Touch," he says as he draws back a ragged shirt, exposing the ulcerating sores of leprosy, "touch and care." We have to ask ourselves in the words of one of our hymns, "Did Christ o'er sinners weep, and shall our tears be dry?"

Who will answer for the lost millions of America? Who will answer for our failure to see, hear, and touch with Christlike compassion the sights and sounds and sores of lost humanity? Who will answer for the stupefying highs of a "good trip" and the horrifying lows of a "bad trip"? Who will answer for the needles, the bottles, the pills with which thousands are destroying the last traces of the image of God in themselves? Who will answer for streams that stink and rivers that are fouled with the excretions of the pollutors of planet Earth? Who will answer for air full of noxious poisons that hang ominously in low, gray, cancerous clouds over our cities?

Who will answer for the mind-blowing, heart-stopping guilt for babies who never asked to be born? Who will answer for marriages easily made and even more easily broken? Who will answer for poverty in an affluent society—poverty that damns the lives of capable and contributing citizens, making them the victims of crime, disease, and ignorance? Who will answer for corruption in government that infiltrates every layer of political life, from the city hall to the United States Congress? Who will answer for the unholy ambitions for political and economic power? Who will answer for the known and unknown Watergates that make a mockery of the government of the people, for the people, and by the people?

Who will answer for loveless churches that turn their backs on human tragedy? Who will answer for preachers silent in the presence of injustice? Who will answer for churches where the pulpit diet is a strange mixture of gospel slogans and civil religion to the neglect of love, justice, mercy, and hope? Who will answer for the millions born and unborn upon whom the light of that cross outside of Jerusalem will never fall? Who will answer for the thousands born to Christless shrouds and Christless graves? Who will answer for persons for whom Christ died? Who will answer for the eternally lost in a hell of guilt and lovelessness now and lost forever in a hell of remorse and regret and refusal?

The only answer to these questions is that we will answer. We will answer because we have not let him touch our eyes, our ears, our hands so that we can see, hear, and touch them in his name. We have not let ourselves come alive to the world through his eyes, his ears, and his hands.

See Paul tossing on that sleepless bed in Troas, with the weight of a world upon him. On that bed in Troas, one man sees a vision, hears a cry and, in Philippi a short time later, he touches the life of a devout woman who becomes the corresponding secretary of the first missionary society that is committed to evangelizing the world. It has been repeated often, but not too often, that the glue that holds Southern Baptists together must be the glue of a burning compassion for evangelism and missions.

In theology, in salvation, in Christian testimony and missions, our texts testify it is the three senses that count. The love of God becomes real only when he sees, he hears, and he touches. The whole renewal movement in the late sixties and the Jesus revolution in the early seventies were a search for a "sensate" faith. A faith that can be seen, heard, and touched became, for the "now" generation, the only real and lasting faith. The meaning of the incarnation is found only in the God who becomes "flesh" and wears our shoes, seeing human agony and ecstasy, hearing our cries, and touching our joys and our sorrows. In missions it is our ability to see, hear, touch, and to react to what we have seen, heard, and touched that identifies us as "his people." To react in faith, hope, and love to the needs of the whole man lost in the physical, mental, social, and spiritual cul-de-sacs of modern life is the epitome of Bold Mission.

We have been seen by him; we have been heard by him; we have been touched by him. Now we must—every one of us—see and hear and touch the lostness of modern man with compassion, understanding, and Christlike love. A recovery of the three senses of mission begins when we become aware of our blindness, our deafness, and our insensitivity. The recovery of the three senses of mission will spur our evangelistic and missionary activity. No pastor, no church, or no denomination becomes spiritually old who retains the three senses of mission.

Seeing God's World

Missions is seeing clearly the world in which we live. The Christian who sees through the eyes of God does not see the world in the same way that others see the world. It we look at the world through the eyes of writers and yesterday's news reports, we will probably see the world pessimistically. You can see the world with Camus in *The Fall* as a soggy hell, like the Zuider Zee where all space is colorless and life is dead, where everlasting nothingness is made visible. You can see the world as a hell of incompatibility with Jean-Paul Sartre in *No Exit*, where the world is a hell of consuming hatreds between a mindless nymphomaniac, a vengeful lesbian, and an impotent male coward who are forced to live together with "no exit." You can see the world as a hell of loneliness with T. S. Eliot in *The Cocktail Party*, and hear Edward, the hollow-hearted socialite, cry out, "Hell is one's self. Hell is alone. Others are only projections of the hell inside us. There is nothing to escape from, and there is nothing to escape with."

We can see the world realistically as a yawning abyss of corruption that opens up in everyday life and invades our own hearts and homes. It exists within us all in hypocrisy, greed, and violence. Fear, hate, and lust are all a part of this world. It includes even that ultimate perversion, the ICBM, that trembles on a thousand launching pads, waiting only for that power-seeking group that will send them screaming into a thousand world cities, making a reality of hell on earth.

One can also see the world idealistically (although there are few who can muster the courage to do it) and believe that the salvation of scientism is just around the corner. It is hard to believe that the good that is in all of us will finally prevail in the kind of a world we live in.

But what does it mean to see the world as a missionary? What does it mean to see the world through the eyes of God? Seeing the world in this way is to see it redemptively. You remember that Jesus touched a blind man who at the first touch of Jesus saw "men as trees walking." Jesus then touched his eyes a second time, and he saw persons clearly. We need that "second touch" for our eyes, our ears, and our hands to see clearly, hear plainly, and touch meaningfully our lost world, our lost community, and our lost friends. Since we are aware of our blindness, let's go back to Jesus Christ for the second touch. When he touches our eyes, we see the world through the eyes of God and see it in faith, hope, and love. When we see the world through the eyes of faith, we see it as God's world. We see it in the context of John 3:16, "God so loved the world, that He gave His only begotten Son." Seeing the world through the eyes of faith helps us to understand that not only is it worth saving, but also it is capable of being saved. It is to see individual lostness, alienation, and despair and to say, "This can be changed." Drug addiction need not be a part of our culture. Poverty need not be a part of our economic system. People do not have to be strangers to the mercies of God in Jesus Christ.

When we see the world through the eyes of hope, we see it as the new world that God is already working on. We see it in the context of "I saw a new heaven and a new earth." We see it in the context of that statement from the closing book of the Bible that God is "now making all things new." God is working on this new world and everything is on his schedule. His purposes of redemption and restoration have not been frustrated or diverted by the planning and perversion of men or the diversions of demons.

When we see the world through the eyes of love, we see it as alienation. When we see the world through the eyes of love, our hearts cry out to the alienation that we may be his instruments of reconciliation. To see the world through the eyes of love is to see it in light of "God actually making his appeal through us." We realize that we have become a part of the answer, and we have ceased to be a part of the problem. It is then that we become the eyes, ears, and hands of God to hear, to see, and to touch his world that is alienated from him.

Seeing the world as a missionary, through the eyes of God and faith, hope, and love, is to see the world in the person next to us on the plane, the neighbor just across the way, the paper boy and the Avon lady, our sons, our daughters, our parents, who are out of Christ. It is seeing that one human life as a microcosm of the world. That basic spiritual schizophrenia that the Bible calls sin sets a person against himself to form what Mackay has called the "Great Rift." It is that struggle of good and evil that is within the person, society, and cosmos.

Now we know who the enemy is and what he proposes to do in human life, society, and in what Ephesians calls the "heavenlies." We struggle not just with flesh and blood but with "rulers of darkness" and "intelligences in the heavenlies." Suddenly Darth Vader comes alive! Knowing who we are fighting for and what we are fighting against will keep us from being divided by sectional ways of seeing our task and by differing views of biblical inspiration.

Horatio Nelson, the great British naval hero, had a word for his admirals that certainly applies to us today. The great British naval commander was informed about a personal vendetta of two of his admirals. They were fighting over strategy. They were no longer speaking to each other. It is said that Nelson called them aboard the flagship and took them to the rail and pointing out across the water to the enemy's mast just showing above the horizon, he said, "Gentlemen, there is the enemy. Our fighting is with him." The word of Nelson is also a word from God for us. "If God be for us, who can be against us?" God will take care of our enemies if we will take care of his task to carry the gospel to the ends of the earth and to the end of time.

Hearing God's Word

Missions is hearing plainly what God is saying to us. There is no reason to believe he is saying anything really different to us now than he said in those commissions that he left for us in the Gospels. It is significant that there is a commission in each of the four Gospels. Each of those commissions places an emphasis upon a different aspect of the mission of the church to God's world. It is unfortunate that in most missionary and evangelistic thinking, all of the emphasis is placed upon the commission in Matthew's Gospel. This is unfortunate because it leaves out some very significant aspects of the mission. Our failure to see the commission of Jesus to evangelize the world in its wholeness by seeing only one commission results in a truncated kind of evangelism and missions.

To put Matthew's words in terms of modern culture, we would have to say that he is saying to us, "As you go into the world, disciple the ethnics." The Greek word is *ethne*, translated "the nations." To put that commission in the terms of modern culture pours a modern context of the word *nations* into the text. Matthew is speaking of the ethnic dimensions of our task. It is not an "Anglo" church or a "southern" church that we are calling out as heralds. This certainly pours new meaning and new urgency into the task of the Home Mission Board as we respond to the need for reaching the ethnic populations of our great cities. This makes America take on new significance as a mission field. Only in America is it possible to reach all the peoples of the earth. Here is our greatest opportunity to produce local churches reflecting the "many colored [variegated] grace of God in Jesus Christ." This statement represents Ephesian philosophy and theology. It is also very important and significant in the Matthew commission that the most significant verb form is the word *teach*. This puts an emphasis upon the educational aspect of evangelism. The gospel is something that must be taught as well as preached. The whole dimension of Christian ethics is significant at this point. New believers must be taught the ethical dimensions of the gospel.

In Mark's Gospel we have another significant commission. Mark says that our Lord has commanded us to "go into all the world and preach the good news to the whole created order." Every biblical scholar commenting on this verse has pointed out the significant shade of meaning in the Commission in this earliest Gospel. Mark writes the gospel of the Servant, commanding us to "gird on the towel" of the servant to become ministers to man's total life upon planet Earth. It is very significant that in the Gospel of Mark the school of Christ is represented as a peripatetic clinic in ministering to the total needs of man. This brings into sharp focus the ministries of the programs at the Home Mission Board and in the state conventions that involve ministry to the moral, physical, mental, and social needs of persons. We do have a ministry to the whole created order of things. Redemption and reconciliation are words that apply not only to man's relationship to God, but also to his relationship to his fellows and to nature and to things. To remember this dimension of the commission of our Lord in Mark's Gospel is to keep us from polarizing ourselves into a "preaching only" kind of missions and evangelism.

For Luke's commission it is necessary for us to put together what he remembered our Lord as saying in his gospel and also in the Acts. When we do this, we have, "You shall be my witnesses." Repentance and the forgiveness of sins must be preaching beginning at Jerusalem, to Judea, Samaria, and the ends of the earth—"this same Jesus you see go away will come again." Luke sets out the terms of the gospel as being forgiveness upon the basis of repentance. The rebel must lay down his arms and surrender to Jesus Christ. There is a real emphasis upon *kerugma*, the preaching of the gospel, in Luke's Gospel and also in the Acts. We are to go into all the frontiers as witnesses—the frontiers of the great cities, the frontiers of the world religions, the frontiers of ethnicity, and to the ends of the earth. We are driven by the urgency of his commission to complete his mission to the ends of the earth and to the end of time. We are not only driven to Judea, Samaria, and the uttermost parts of the earth, but we are also driven to the end of time at the return of our Lord. With Luke the word is immediacy and urgency. It is necessary that the message be preached and proclaimed to all men everywhere. There is no time to waste.

John's Gospel really puts all things together for us when he says to us in the words of our Lord, "As the Father sent me, in the same way and on the same mission I send you" (see John 17:18). There is only one kind of church in the New Testament. The church is missionary. It is unfortunate that we have to talk about certain churches as being missionary and other churches as being evangelistic. We even write books on the subject of the missionary church or the evangelistic church. The truth is, there is only one kind of church. It is both evangelistic and missionary. A church that fails at the point of missions and evangelism is a church that fails to be a church at all. Missions is not just one of the many things a church must do. It is what the church must do. Evangelism is not just one of the many messages that the church bears. It is the message that the church bears. In light of this, our commitments of time, money, and persons to missions must come under the compulsion of this commission. It is not possible for a church to set priorities above missions and evangelism. It is unfortunate that many churches which cry out loudly about being a missionary or an evangelistic church in terms of their budget and time are really not committed to missions and evangelism at all.

Touching Man's Need

Missions and evangelism is touching in the name of Jesus Christ the deepest human needs in the power of his Holy Spirit and touching them with compassion and understanding. Touching evolves logically from seeing God's world and hearing God's word. The Bible is plain when it says, "But prove yourselves doers of the word, and not merely hearers who delude themselves" (Jas. 1:22). When we minister to a person's spiritual, moral, physical, and mental needs, we need to remember that we are not just ministering to a person but we are actually ministering to Jesus Christ. "Truly I say to you, to the extent that you did it to one of the these brothers of Mine, even the least of them, you did it to Me" (Matt. 25:40).

Missions is touching in the name of Jesus Christ the needs of a person next door or thousands of miles away across the ocean. How do you reach from Atlanta to the Bronx or to Muleshoe, Texas? For that matter, how do you reach from those hands scarred with nails, and that voice made hoarse from fever and thirst, and those ears so blasted by derision and mockery—how do you reach from him to human hearts?

When Jesus Christ, who received by giving and who ruled by serving and who lived by dying, left this world, he left us a legacy of only two things: a band of evangelizers and a church. He did not even leave a New Testament for the bank of evangelizers. The church lived and worked for four centuries without a canon of Scripture. The band of evangelizers soon learned that the base of their operations was that church that he spoke into existence at Caesarea-Philippi.

Isn't this still the way, the strategy? A band of evangelizers fellowshipping in a church which is his body. The church is his eyes to see, his ears to hear, and his hands to touch. Doesn't this make evangelism and missions come alive? What is our priority task? What has been the priority in Bold Mission? It is planting churches and developing each church into a band of evangelizers.

Does this flesh out for you our task? We are not just talking about a Home Mission Board and Cooperative Program and Annie Armstrong Easter Offering. We are now talking about a band of evangelizers in the church.

That is how you get from Atlanta to the Bronx and to Muleshoe, Texas. That is how you get from that one on the cross who bared forever the heart that loves those who hate him to the last lost soul. You reach that unchurched community through a band of evangelizers and a church. You plant churches and you train and equip a band of evangelizers. That is our commitment. That is the essence of Bold Mission. That is the reason we made evangelism into a section and church extension and language missions into divisions at the Home Mission Board.

A band of evangelizers working in and through and out of a church is all that we have to accomplish our tasks. Everything else that we have, including agencies, institutions, commissions, computers, secretaries, typewriters, buildings, is meaningless and useless unless it supports that legacy that he left us.

With his last dying breath, he told us what to do. All we need to do is be obedient. How we do it is really not that important. We really don't need to know how. It is the will we need—the will ribbed and edged with steel. When he told that early church to go and evangelize the world, they simply went out and did what he told them to do. This is our greatest need today. It is to understand clearly what he said for us to do and to get about doing it. There is no time to wait and waste. We must be about our task.

With his last dying breath, he told us what to do. Let's recover our spiritual eyesight so that we can lead others to see the truth. Let's open our ears so that others can hear Jesus and his words of life. Let's touch man's needs and bring the healing hand of Jesus to the hurting world. Let's do it because he told us to do it and because to fail to do it is treason to our Lord.

Has it been so long ago and far away that we have forgotten? Have we forgotten that bloody man who hung between heaven and earth on a skull-shaped hill outside Jerusalem? Have we forgotten what he told us to do first, last, and always? Have we forgotten the vision of a new world in the morning? Do we have to ask in the words of Wordsworth, "Whither is fled the visionary gleam? Where is it now, the glory and the dream?"

The visionary dream is still there. The glory and the dream are still there. The vision, the glory, and the dream were his. He left them with us. Some of the brothers in the early church wrote them down under the inspiration of the Holy Spirit. They are still with us for us to read and to share the vision, the glory, and the dream. Our final word in this chapter is a prayer from Kipling, "Lord of Hosts, be with us yet, lest we forget, lest we forget."

5
Go Quickly and Tell

On that cold foreboding night when man murdered, three women were the last to leave the garden tomb. Mary of Magdala, Mary, the mother of James, and Salome were there when two rich men brought the body of our Lord to the garden. It is strange that the one who loved the poor so dearly should be ministered to by two rich men in the ancient rites of the Jews. The women waited while two men with the assistance of their servants washed the sweat- and blood-stained body. While they talked in whispers, the ministers of love pressed spices and myrrh into the five blue-black gaping wounds and carefully wound the body in linen winding sheets. They heard the two men chant the funeral psalm that they knew so well. They knew that the funeral psalm having been sung each of the men would kiss his forehead and cover his face with soft linen. The women saw them emerge from the tomb and push the stone already shaped for a door into place, and the tomb was sealed. The three stalwarts sobbing quietly saw the men leave. They lingered. (See John 19.)

Nothing earthly could shake off the sense of depression the women felt because of the darkness of that cold night and the awful fate of their Lord. The Son of God crucified like a common criminal. Their Messiah not sitting on a throne but lying in a tomb. Their hearts had lifted when on Sunday he had been hailed as a king riding on the foal of an ass. Now on the eve of the sabbath next he was dead. They remained in the cold dark night, huddled together for warmth and for solace, the only despairing survivors of a broken cause. They talked. They wept. They prayed. They tried recalling some of his words and some of the things he did. They retold the incidents when he brought the dead to life. They remembered again the woman with the issue of blood and the son of the widow of Nain. They heard once more the Aramaic words, "Talitha cumi," and saw the dead daughter rise up and walk. Finally the chill and the unholy darkness drove them away as well, and the garden tomb was alone with the angels and the Father.

They left him in his grave Friday evening just before the sabbath. His dead body, hastily entombed, was wrapped in winding sheets that enclosed a hundred weight of balms and spices. The tomb was closed and the heavy door guarded by two centurions.

Then came Sunday morning.[1] It was the same garden but strangely different. The heaviness of despair was gone. In the tomb of the rich man, Joseph of Arimathea, there was a strange stirring, a presence of unseen powers and forces. Something from the beyond, something far beyond the understanding of the earthbound was at work. The breath of God rustled the leaves of the olive trees and moved the heavy stone. Strong, immeasurable, and mighty forces poured life into the dead body. He is alive! He sits up and the graveclothes fall away. He walks out into the moonlit garden. No one has seen except the angels and they cannot tell. Who will tell the good news? Our Lord is not dead, he is alive! Who will tell? Will kings be the first to bear the good news? Will robed ecclesiastics be the first to tell the world that he is alive? Will angels write the words "he is risen" across the sky, using a fiery comet as a pen?

The first rosy streaks of the dawn of the first day of the week already are appearing in the east. They light the way for the three women returning to the tomb. They were the last to leave, and they are the first to return. One of the women says to the others, "Look, the stone is rolled away." The others peer through the light of the new coming day and indeed the stone had been rolled away and on the stone was an angel clothed in light. Matthew tells the story.

Now late on the Sabbath, as it began to dawn toward the first day of the week, Mary Magdalene and the other Mary came to look at the grave. And behold, a severe earthquake had occurred, for an angel of the Lord descended from heaven and came and rolled away the stone and sat upon it. And his appearance was like lightning, and his garment white as snow; and the guards shook for fear of him, and became like dead men. And the angel answered and said to the women, "Do not be afraid; for I know that you are looking for Jesus who has been crucified. He is not here, for He has risen, just as He said. Come, see the place where He was lying. And go quickly and tell His disciples that He has risen from the dead" (Matt. 28:1-7).

The angel gave to the women the first gospel message, the gospel of the resurrection. "Go quickly and tell." Why were the women the last to leave and the first to arrive at the garden tomb? Why were the women the first to receive the gospel of the resurrection? Doesn't my first question really answer the last? They were the first to be commissioned to tell because they were the last to leave and the first to return. They stayed longer and returned sooner because they loved more. Their concern would not let them stay away. While the men were returning to business as usual, the women were returning to the tomb. There is great biblical precedent for women being in the forefront of mission. Women were the last at the cross and the first at the tomb. Women were given the first command to tell the gospel of the resurrection. A woman was the first person to preach the gospel to the Jews (Luke 2:37-38). Women were prominent in attending the first great prayer meeting in which the church was born (Acts 1:14). The first persons in Europe to receive the gospel were women (Acts 16:14). A woman was immortalized by Christ who said she would be remembered wherever the gospel is preached (Luke 10:42).

The word *missions* is almost synonymous with *women*. Paul's first mission thrust into Europe gained converts among devout women. The first secretary of Christian world missions may well have been Lydia of Thyatira, the seller of purple. A business-woman of the first century becomes a missions executive. Every sacrifice and heroic pioneering ever done by David Livingstone can be matched and surpassed by "Ma" Slessor of Calabar. What would Southern Baptist missions have been without the vision and leadership of our women? When the men of the Southern Baptist Convention lacked the vision and the love to support missions, the women sent their "egg" money to the support of our first missionaries. We have never really paid tribute to those thousands of Southern Baptist women who have opted for the single life for the love of Christ. Lovely, kind, and definitely mar- riageable, they have renounced husbands, children, and homes for his mission. We salute them.

What is woman on mission? Christian woman on mission is "Ma" Slessor opening the dark continent before Livingstone. Christian woman on mission is Lillian Carter crying and sobbing by a roadside in India trying to feed a leper whose whole body is filled with ulcerating sores. While she is feeding the leper, she is being cursed by a doctor for prolonging her life. Christian woman on mission is Anne Sullivan whose "miracle at the pumphouse" was a miracle of patient Christian love that opened the windows of a great creative mind and gave the world Helen Keller. Chris- tian woman on mission is Ann Judson, desperately ill on the *Ille De France* on January 12, 1812, pouring her tears, love, and devotion on the pages of a diary that throb with love for Jesus Christ. Christian woman on mission is Vivia Perpetua, dying in the Roman Coliseum on the horns of a wild beast and crying out her love for Jesus Christ and urging the spectators to receive him as Lord. Time does not allow us to talk about Annie Armstrong, Lottie Moon, Thelma Frith Bagby, Alma Hunt, Carolyn Weath- erford, and the thousands of others who witness, labor, and love on his mission.

Four Resurrection Imperatives

The women are to believe and not be afraid. This is the first of four imperatives in this passage. They are urged to look at the evidence—the stone rolled away, the empty tomb, and the con- dition of the graveclothes. Now that they have seen they are urged not to be afraid. What they saw was so staggering that it was beyond human belief. It required faith. Our hesitation in refusing to believe what seems to be true is dispelled only when we take him at his word. God's "Look, I have told you," is his last word to us. The gates of the grave had closed behind him and upon his disciples had fallen the shadow of death. But these women still loved him, and love is stronger than death. They loved; they believed; and they had hope. He is risen. "But now abide faith, hope, love, these three; but the greatest of these is love" (1 Cor. 13:13). These first missioners of the good news were the first to believe his resurrection.

The second imperative is to share. "Go tell," is the Great Commission in two words. The first impulse of those who believe his resurrection is to tell others the good news. The woman at the well of Samaria is another instance of a woman who became an instant missionary to her own hometown. She went through the streets telling others, "Come see a man who told me everything I have ever done" (see John 4:29). She was one of the first evangelists to the cities. The Christian life is living a life worth sharing and sharing a life worth living. Many years ago a young woman served as a missionary in the Haymarket in Louisville, Kentucky. She was known as "the angel of the Haymarket." She walked in the streets sharing her faith in Christ with the hurting, the hopeless, and the helpless. She was never insulted or assaulted. The human wreckage she witnessed to seemed to sense that the "angel" was different. There are more than 80 million non-Christians waiting for "the angel" on their street to share. There are 7 million alcoholics, 1.4 million nonreaders, and a half of a million non-Christian religionists waiting for someone to share.

The third imperative is rejoice. The Greek word is *chairete* and it means to exult. This was the word of greeting used by the risen Savior to the women, but literally it means "to rejoice." It was used by the victor in the Greek games and can mean "victory." There was cause to rejoice, for the dark, cold, unholy blackness of the night before had given way to the rosy light of the day of resurrection. Jesus Christ is victor over death, hell, and the grave. We need to revive the art of holy exulting. He puts light into blinded eyes and laughter on lips silenced by sadness. He sets the star of hope on the black bosom of our night with the morning light and now he rebuilds the fires of faith in three human hearts and tells them to "rejoice." Annie Johnson Flint in her poem "May Joy Be Thine" expresses well this legacy of resurrection joy passed on to us by these women.

> The Easter joy be thine:
> The joy of those who, weeping
> Because their dead in straitened chambers sleeping,
> Have left them for a while,
> Yet know that loosed from all earth's tribulations
> They have passed on to heavenly habitations,
> To life eternal and the Father's smile;
> The joy of those who hear
> Beyond all doubt and fear,
> Though jarring echoes of discordant strife,
> That one Voice sounding clear
> "I am the Resurrection and the Life;
> They who believe on Me
> From death's dark thrall I free;
> I drank that bitter cup, I passed that gloomy door,
> Through that lone valley I have gone before
> Because I live, they live forevermore.
> This joy be thine."[1]

The last of the resurrection imperatives given to the women was "Go." In relation to missions we think of the word *go* in terms of a missionary going to a home or foreign field. In terms of today's missionary we think about moving vans, language school, and new places to see. In terms of millions of Christian women who will never do that it means something else. I think Nell Tyner Bowen was speaking what I am thinking about when she wrote:

> Lord,
> Thank you for involving yourself personally and
>   intimately with me.
> You are love
> From now on, through your life within me, I am
> turned to "go" for personal and intimate
>   involvement with you.
> To experience

To return
To reflect
Your love.[2]

   The kind of "go" we are thinking about is best expressed by the slang expression, "I am sitting on ready." Paul expressed it very well, "So, much as in me is, I am ready to preach the gospel to you that are at Rome also." This kind of "go" is a fine-tuned spiritual preparation that makes us available to God. The women were the first evangels of the resurrection gospel because they wanted to be near. They were there. In the frantic and often frenetic world we live in it is difficult for us to live close to God. The success of early Southern Baptist missions was due to the spiritual resources of thousands of praying, teaching, and influential women. It was no different in the New Testament. Read the last chapter of Romans and take note of the many feminine names in the roll call of those who labored in the missionary journeys of Paul. These women were "standing on go." They were ready to pray, to give, to go, to witness, or whatever God had for them. If we were writing an "epistle to the Atlantans" today, we could write about "these women who have labored in the gospel." Most of them are unknown, unsung, and unselfish.

My Program Is Love

   "What is your program?" the Russian seaman demanded. Fern Powers answered, "Love." "Free love?" the seaman asked. "No," she replied, "God love." Fern Powers is a woman on mission and her mission is evangelism. She is the dynamo providing the spiritual energies for the Harbor evangelistic ministry in Olympia, Washington. The ministry was born in the warm heart and creative mind of this wife-grandmother-career woman who keeps house, takes a daughter to school and to guitar lessons, and who sometimes weeds the garden. Albert, Alex, and David were three Buddhist seamen from the ship *World Champion* out of Hong Kong. Fern invited them to a Sunday evening church service and to a meal in the Powers's home after the service. She was surprised when it turned out that it was the evening for the

Lord's Supper observance. The three men thought that the grape juice and the small pieces of bread were the promised meal. Albert thought the small portions were funny and he began laughing. Fern explained to him what it meant and that the meal would come afterward in her home. Albert was shocked and asked, "Have I offended your God?"

"No," she replied. "Ours is a God of love."

"Then, I too want to become a Christian," Albert said. He was the first convert of the evangelistic mission to the seamen.

Albert started a Bible study on his ship and constantly wrote Fern reporting his progress and asking for advice in sharing his faith. Fern can show you some pictures of Albert, his wife, and his new baby. The pictures and correspondence are evidence that this seaman's ministry does more than count as converts everyone who agrees with a presentation of the gospel. Fern and the others from the First Baptist Church, Lacey, Washington, who are a part of the ministry follow up those who profess conversion and sometimes at great personal effort. Alex, one of the other Buddhist guests that evening, called one evening after Fern had returned from work as an accountant assistant. Alex was in Coos Bay 400 miles away on the coast of Oregon. He told Fern how disappointed he was that the ship was not coming into Olympia. Fern and her husband Bill took Bonnie their daughter and drove late into the night to Coos Bay. They searched for a motel room along the way and could not find a vacancy. They slept in the car along the beach, ate breakfast, and then sought out the ship Alex was on. Alex, standing on the rail, spotted Bonnie's red hair. Fern says, "He whooped and hollered and ran down to us. He couldn't believe we came all that way to see him." Many ports later Alex wrote them, "When I return, I shall make the march for Christ."

What does all this hectic pace and lack of privacy do for the family? Bill, the husband and father, stays in the background but he is very supportive. He is a hunter-fisherman employed in civil service. He makes friends with many of the seamen and keeps Fern's car running. He bails out Fern in emergencies. One cold

damp morning a trip to take seamen to Mount Ranier depended
on his getting chains on the car which he did with only good-
humored complaining. Fern says that the three married children,
Dale Ann, Boyd, and Verna have not had much contact with the
ministry with seamen but she believes Bonnie and Kelly are more
mission-minded as a result of the ministry. Bill admits that sometimes the constant going and the lack of privacy are difficult. They
all seem to agree that "the program" of God-love is rewarding and
worthwhile.

The First Baptist Church of Lacey has for the most part ac-
cepted the seamen as a part of their ministry. Pastor Harry Han-
nah says that the seamen's ministry seldom pays off in new
members, and then adds, "The church is not here to see how fast
it can grow—but for service." Fern believes that the pastor's support and attitude is a major factor in the success of the program
of love. The pastor says that the seamen's ministry has made the
church aware of ethnic groups living in the community. The
church has employed a Korean, Pastor Cho, who is fluent in
other Oriental languages. Some of the Oriental families attend
the services of the First Baptist Church. Fern's unbelievable energies of love have reached out to other groups. She was instru-
mental in leading the church in working with Vietnamese refugees.

With no theological training and with only a Berlitz dictionary,
a parallel Bible, and sometimes with no words at all, Fern and
other members of the First Baptist Church of Lacey articulate
love that cuts through the barriers of class, culture, and language. They communicate love that crosses the barriers of
Oriental theology and the Iron Curtain of communism. The
Northwest Convention gives forty dollars per month toward
twelve tanks of gasoline that the ministry requires. One denominational leader said of this ministry, "It is unbelievable. The
sheer energy expended is unbelievable. The fact that they have
not grown tired of it is unbelievable. Their consistency is unbelievable. The fact that it doesn't require great amounts of money
is unbelievable." Fern tries to explain the driving force for all this

by saying, "There is something in me, I think, that—that just reaches out to them. I—I love these people. I love every minute of this work. I just do."

Evangelism is the first guideline of the Home Mission Board, and Fern Powers incarnates evangelistic love reaching out to others. A woman demonstrates for all of us what it means to share the love of Christ with others. She teaches us that the language of love is more important in crossing barriers between us and others than linguistic skills. She tells us that the lack of money is no reason for failing to be on mission. She is telling us that our being busy in a career, or as a housewife, or as a worker in the church need not keep us from obeying him in sharing our love. When evangelism is on the priority with us as it is in the life of Fern Powers, our churches will be revolutionized, our denomination will be revitalized, and our nation will be evangelized.

I Am Coming In

"The Wall" is the popular name for the Virginia Penitentiary. A massive barrier environs the compound to heights of fifty feet. The prison is like a fortress very close to downtown Richmond. Very early one spring morning a slender angular woman in her fifties stood before the heavy grey bars of a cell-block gate. The guard was very firm, "I can't let you in." The woman's voice was hard and her words very sharp and crisp, "I am coming in. You call the warden, or your lieutenant, and call him now, because I'm coming in there." The guard thought about her words briefly, pulled the lever, and opened the gate. A woman chaplain in a maximum security prison? The Chaplaincy Service entirely supported by the churches of Virginia provides the chaplains for the prison system of the state. When the chaplain at The Wall resigned over a conflict with the warden, Marjorie Bailey was appointed the new chaplain. Marjorie has a sense of humor and when asked about her new job she said, "What old maid wouldn't like to have 950 men all to herself?"

Marjorie, a Southern Baptist, makes the word *ministry* take on new meaning for us. She makes the words, "I was in prison and you visited me," a living reality. Marjorie still serves as chaplain at the women's prison at Goochland as well as at The Wall. On her second day at The Wall she tells how she was approached by "a great big dude." He said, "The Press says you got two jobs. Are you getting more money coming here?" She looked him straight in the eyes and said, "Mister, there's not enough money in the US to pay me to be chaplain to this penitentiary." He nodded his head and said, "We are going to watch you and see how you do." An inmate was asked if Marjorie was in danger in case of a prison riot. He said that if there was a prison riot or strike they would probably turn to Marjorie as a negotiator because they trusted her.

Because Marjorie has been at Goochland, the women's prison, longer, she feels more freedom there. She says, "I am a different person here." The campus-like look at Goochland is a contrast to the forbidding grayness of The Wall. An inmate poet at Goochland put the loneliness and frustration of prison life into verse. Julie Mulik wrote:

> The loneliness so heavy,
> Falls down on my head,
> But all I can do is sit on my bed
> And think of death, where there is no thought
> Or routine, or guards, or life being led,
> In a prison where I wish I were dead!

Julie Mulik became a Christian at Goochland and her pessimism and despair turned to joy and she wrote a poem she called "Miss Bailey's Smile." She closes the poem with,

> Your smile is sunshine,
>   It brightens up the day.
> So let me frame your smile,
>   And share it along the way.

Marjorie carries a key at Goochland, a key that hangs by a cord around her neck. She carries another key in her heart. It is a key that says, "I am coming in." She enlists volunteers from the

Virginia WMU and other women's church groups to assist her in her ministry at Goochland. On Sundays she is joined by choir members, the choir director, and others who are interested from the First Baptist Church of Maniken. Marjorie's commitment to the gospel is evident in what she says to the inmates in the service. "Many of you told me that life here is hell. (Amens) There is a hell much worse than this for those who do not know the power of the resurrection." She calls for open living of the faith and closes with, "If you have a need for prayer, come."

Marjorie Bailey incarnates another word that underlines the work of The Home Mission Board. That word is *ministry*. The same One who came and spoke to the women at the tomb is the One who said, "I did not come to be ministered to, but to minister, and give my life." That is the key that opens the door of loneliness, frustration, and defeat and says, "I am coming in." Many doors that are closed to a bold presentation of the gospel on first encounter are opened by loving ministry. Paul, the great missionary evangelist, said that "without love" (ministry is love in action), our message is like "a noisy gong or clanging cymbal." A valid question for all of us and all of our churches is: What is our ministry? If our mission is Christlike, it must include ministry.

On the Way, By the Way

If you ask Faye Pierce, Sunday School teacher at Spring Hill Baptist Church in Mobile, Alabama, how to share your Christian faith, she answers, "On the way, in the way, and oh, by the way." Faye says that you have opportunities to witness when you are on the way to do something else if you will only see them. She is on her way to do something all of the time. She is the wife of a Mobile attorney, mother of four children, and a Southern Baptist Interfaith Witness associate. She is a volunteer. Voluntarily she has equipped herself to witness. Voluntarily she witnesses to persons of other faiths. Voluntarily she informs other Southern Baptists about the opportunities to witness to persons of other religious faiths. In addition to all of this she teaches psychology at the University of South Alabama, plays tennis, and is active at the Country Club. But on the way, in the way, and "Oh, by the way," she is a witness for her faith.

Faye incarnates another great word. That word is *witness*. She has many friends in the Unification Church and among Roman Catholics. She does not hesitate to refer to the Unification Church as a cult, yet she looks constantly for a common experience in Christ. She believes in studying Roman Catholicism firsthand. She goes to priests and nuns for instruction. On the other hand she believes they need to know about Southern Baptists firsthand. The leader of a Catholic young people's class invited Faye to speak. They were going to show a film about what Southern Baptists believe. She asked, "Who produced the film?" They said, "Catholics." She said, "Let's not show it because Catholics think a certain way about Baptists. Let me talk. If there are questions, I will answer them." She had prepared a New Testmant for each member of the class. Each copy had the plan of salvation marked. She told them, "A lot of you want to know what it means to have a religious experience as a Baptist and this is what we believe." She then took them verse by verse through the plan of salvation.

Faye gets excited about witnessing to "Moonies" on the street. She says that very often they refuse any conversation. She says, "Theologically speaking they are dead wrong," but she insists that showing them Christian kindness is very important. She reminds her Sunday School class as she teaches at Spring Hill, "Sharing Christ along the way in life may mean sharing with a Moonie selling candy as he passes through a store or shopping center. It may mean not buying the candy, but telling them that if they ever need a friend you will help. Just say, 'My name is so-and-so and I love you in the name of Christ.' " Demonstrating that her concern is for all people she has worked with migrant workers and poor expectant mothers. Her evaluation of all this witnessing activity and ministry is, "I feel like God has said for me to get ready to do this work. I'm just waiting to see where he is going to send me."

A dream of the evangelism section of the Home Mission Board has been to inspire, train, and equip thousands of Southern Baptist laypersons for witness ministry. Interfaith Witness is attempting to equip thousands of laypersons for open, intelligent, sharing witness to persons of other religious faiths. The need exists in every church for every community. Faye makes witness take on flesh and blood. She shows us that to be a volunteer all you need to do is volunteer. When we count missionaries, we do not count Faye Pierce, but she is a missionary. When we count evangelists, we do not count Faye Pierce, but she is an evangelist. When we count ministers, we do not count Faye Pierce, but she is a minister. I think God counts her, too. If Southern Baptists had 50,000 volunteers like Faye Pierce, we might just turn things around for the Lord.

She Tells Them the Truth

Roosevelt "Big Daddy" Nivens is the football coach at Langston University, a predominantly black college in Central Oklahoma. He says of the black student today, "One thing about black kids nowadays, they are looking for something real. On this campus the students are aware of a lot of jive." Then he says of Verlene Farmer and her relationship to the students, "They don't want jive. They just want the truth. And she tells them the truth." Verlene Farmer is a teacher. She serves as BSU director and Bible teacher at Langston. Verlene has heard the Lord say, "Go and tell." Nivens, the football coach, became involved in the BSU program five years ago after being inspired by Farmer. The huge athlete weighing 290 pounds says that in those five years she has been responsible for 75 football players accepting Christ. "She knows how to talk to these kids . . . how to tell them about Jesus . . . she tells them the truth; she don't put no sugar on it." Verlene incarnates another great word for missions, the word *teach*.

In her second year as a student at Langston, Verlene fell in love with a fine young man whose health had been damaged as a prisoner of the Communists during the Korean conflict. She became one of two black young women chosen to integrate the Carver School of Missions at Southern Seminary. On a missions day she made a commitment to missions that ruled out marriage. She had to call her fine young man and tell him. She says, "I cried my tears and went on to the mission field. He got married and stayed here." She served for a time in Liberia but had to return because of toxic hepatitis in 1966. She is not bitter but the remarks of students at Carver when she was there as the first black to attend still hurt. In 1971 she returned to Langston to teach and serve as BSU director.

Verlene has no problem with attention in the classroom. Straight and slim she stands before the class, a wide bright smile wrinkling the nose under gold-framed glasses and etching laugh lines around her mouth and eyes. Animation and austerity are part of her teaching style. Ada Fisher, the first black woman to enter the University of Oklahoma law school and chairman of the department of social sciences at Langston, says of Verlene, "She's one of the most enthusiastic and conscientious teachers we have." With a sly smile Fisher points out the door between her office and Farmer's classroom: "Sometimes I crack the door a little and listen to her teach." Farmer says of herself, "I'm just going on my way. I'm a fuddy-duddy, but we need some fuddy-duddies in this world today. We need some more fuddy-duddies who know what they believe. . . . We don't need somebody who says, 'I think this is what the Bible says,' we need somebody who says, 'I know what the Bible says.' " Verlene is still telling the truth at Langston, and young men and women are coming to Christ because she is a teacher.

These four women epitomize the wide and varied ministries of the Home Mission Board.[3] *Evangelize, witness, minister,* and *teach* are electric words that are our way of doing what the angel of the Lord told the three women at the empty tomb, "Go quickly and tell." You may be saying, "But I am not a Fern Powers or Faye Pierce or Marjorie Bailey or Verlene Farmer." No, you are not, but you are you and within you is the ability to volunteer to go quickly and tell. Your mission field is all around you. Fern found hers in the busy harbor at her back door. Faye has found hers in her world of going. Marjorie has found hers behind the walls of prisons. Verlene found hers in the classroom. Yours is right around you somewhere. Pray that he will open your eyes to see the hurt that needs to be healed, or the ignorance that needs to be dispelled, or the mind that needs to be taught. How will you do it? Love will find a way.

What is the relationship of the three women by the empty tomb almost two millenniums ago and the four women who have been our parables in this chapter? All of the women heard the same voice say the same words, "Go quickly and tell." The same voice, the same message, the same urgency through almost two thousand years of Christian missions. Some still hear and go. Some still hear and refuse to go. Some are so busy that they never hear. The work of the mission goes on. Sometimes it is unbearably difficult and slow. Sometimes it is incredibly easy and fast. Whether we find the going difficult or easy, the mission must go on. The message must go out. He is alive. It is the gospel of the resurrection. Tell it now. Tell it everywhere. Tell it, on the way, in the way, and "Oh, by the way." Thank you, Fern Powers. Thank you, Faye Pierce. Thank you, Marjorie Bailey. Thank you, Verlene Farmer. Thank you every truth-telling, love-sharing, life-giving volunteer.

Notes

1. See Peter Marshall, *Mr. Jones, Meet the Master* (New York: Fleming H. Revell Company, 1950), pp. 104 ff.

2. Annie Johnson Flint, *Poems*, Vol. 2 (Toronto: Evangelical Publishers, 1948), p. 41.

3. Nell Tyner Bowen, *The Seeking Woman I Am* (Who Press, 1978), p. 63.

4. The material on Fern Powers, Faye Pierce, Marjorie Bailey, and Verlene Farmer is from the Home Mission Board books, *Road to Reconciliation*, *American Montage*, *Your God, My God*, and *Love on the Line* and is used by permission.

6
Prerequisites for Bold Mission

In a recent television commercial an obviously precocious little boy is being interviewed by a newsman. The boy is sitting on his front steps looking pensively across the street. "What are you going to do when you grow up?" the newsman asks. The boy replies, "I am going to drive an automobile. I am going to fly a plane. I am going to drive a train." Then he pauses a moment in deep thought and adds, "As soon as my mother lets me cross the street." That young man is exactly right. There are some prerequisites to driving automobiles, flying planes, and driving trains. You have to learn how to cross the street on foot. There are some things that are so basic to action that they may be forgotten in the first flush of wanting to do something.

Southern Baptists have committed themselves to Bold Mission—a goal of giving every person the opportunity to hear and respond to the gospel and every person the opportunity to be a part of a New Testament fellowship of believers by the year 2000. Thirty-five thousand churches, more than 35,000 pastors and denominational leaders, several great agencies, 35 state conventions, and 1,200 associations have geared up for a push into the future. All of us have been challenged to lay it on the line in making Bold Mission the greatest thrust by any group of evangelicals since the days of the New Testament. The dream of placing 50,000 volunteer missionaries in the field to support the work and ministry of career missionaries is one of the thrilling aspects of Bold Mission. The nature of Bold Mission has been poured into three bold words that thrill us with their potential.

Going is a great word and close to the hearts of Southern Baptists who have always been ardent activists. We are going to places where we have never gone before—to hundreds of counties with no evangelical witness. We are going to the great cities of America—to the jungles of concrete and steel—to the citadels of power and influence—to the breeding ground of poverty and crime. We are going to communities in transition—to communities where Christians are running from fellow Christians—to communities where Christians and churches grope for answers amid brokenness, prejudice, and alienation. We are going to the poor with bread and the Bread of life—to stand in solidarity with them and decry with them the obscenity of their degrading and dehumanizing lot. We are going to those who are broken and hurt by life—the mentally retarded, the nonreaders, the prisoners—to gird on the towel of brotherhood and ministry. We are going to evangelize, to plant churches, to preach, and teach the gospel until all have heard. We are going with a gospel that is an ache in our hearts, a gospel demanding to be shared with the world. Bold going is one aspect of Bold Mission.

Growing is another great word. Growing is a great word for the people of God who have "the kingdom" in their hearts. Growing is a great word for disciples who are now becoming "a new lean breed" of believers who count no cost, consider no odds, and who are ready to gamble their lives on Jesus Christ. Growing is a great word for churches intent on becoming local assemblies of the body of Christ, churches who practice the priesthood of believers, so that every believer is ministering in love to his neighbor. Growing is a great word for pastors who are more and more made in the image of the One who said of himself in the Latin Vulgate version, "I am the good Pastor." Growing is a great word for the increasing numbers of believers baptized into him and into his body, the church, until we can exult in the fact that "like a mighty army moves the church of God."

Giving is the last of the trilogy of words that express Bold Mission. Giving must be a great word to the denomination that grew a generation of tithers who are now financing the greatest missionary thrust since the days of the New Testament church. Giving means giving ourselves to the Lord for salvation from the penalty, power, and presence of sin. Giving means giving ourselves to him in full surrender that brings "the peace that passes all understanding through Jesus Christ our Lord." Giving means for believers giving "the last full measure of devotion" in Christlike sacrificial ministry. Giving means that we have made it possible for every person to hear the gospel and every person to attend a fellowship of believers. Giving means for the church that his mission will have priority over all lesser goals. Giving means that we can boldly say that this is the day of the Lord's deliverance—that we will preach the good news to the poor; we will bind up the brokenhearted; we will heal those who have been beaten and bruised by life; we will preach deliverance to those who are imprisoned by alcohol, drugs, pornography, and mental illness.

Are we really ready for this kind of Bold Mission? Have we learned how to cross the street yet? Are there some biblical requisites for mission that we still have not mastered? It may well be that we want to fly planes, drive trains, and drive automobiles before we have learned how to cross the street. The church in the New Testament had a preparation meeting for world witness that changed the people of God from cringing cowards who denied Christ to bold confessors who affirmed him. The church in the New Testament did not attain its missionary zeal and vision easily. There were battles to be fought against racism, Judaizing fundamentalism, and resistance to change. One thing Satan does not wish the church to be is missionary.

Something happened to the church at the Feast of Pentecost that prepared them for world mission. It was something born of the Holy Spirit that occurred among that little band upon whom the task of world evangelization was to fall. What happened is so basic and fundamental to mission that we must read the very words of the New Testament and hopefully feel again the "wind of the Spirit" that breathed upon that waiting congregation long ago. What that little band would do in the next 20 years would overthrow empires and change the course of history.

When the day of Pentecost had come, they were all together in one place. And suddenly there came from heaven a noise like a violent, rushing wind, and it filled the whole house where they were sitting. And there appeared to them tongues as of fire distributing themselves, and they rested on each one of them. And they were all filled with the Holy Spirit and began to speak with other tongues, as the Spirit was giving them utterance (Acts 2:1-4).

The spiritual experience turned the worshipers into witnesses, and they began witnessing to the great crowds in Jerusalem gathered for the Feast of Pentecost. Peter later that day preached to a great mass of people. Three thousand persons made a commitment to Jesus Christ as Lord and were baptized. The people of God were on mission. The gospel was witnessed to and preached, and Luke the historian of these events says, "And the Lord was adding to their number day by day those who were being saved" (Acts 2:47). Pentecost burned two great words in the heart of the early church, *evangelism* and *missions*. The survival of the Home Mission Board or the presence of the missionary on the frontiers of need in America are not dependent upon the generosity and sacrifice of any one church in giving to the Cooperative Program or to the Annie Armstrong offering. The very existence of any one church as a New Testament church is dependent upon its missionary and evangelistic zeal.

A Baptist church may be in the heart of the Bronx or beside a busy freeway in Houston, but in order to be his church on his mission it must be evangelistic and it must be missionary. A Baptist church may be in the Kentucky mountains or in Atlanta, but if it is to be a New Testament church it must be evangelistic and it must be missionary. The church without New Testament evangelistic zeal and missionary compulsion to reach the person next door and into the farthest reaches of the world "has a name that she lives, but she is dead." The faithful preaching of the gospel and sending out missionaries in the remainder of the Book of Acts resulted in recurring passages from the pen of the historian such as "So the churches were being strengthened in the faith, and were increasing in number daily" (Acts 16:5). If the church is to be on Bold Mission, we must go back to the basics that teach us how to cross the street before we can go to the ends of the earth.

The mission to evangelize and congregationalize the first-century world began in the upper room of Jerusalem where 120 prayed and waited for orders. There is a kind of thrilling primitive simplicity about what happened in Acts that needs to happen in our churches today. There are principles involved in the events at Pentecost that are spiritual laws of renewal and revival that are as unchanging as the orbit of the planets and the nature of God. I believe we need to remind ourselves of these basic principles. We will fail ourselves and we will disappoint our Lord if we do not call ourselves back to the spiritual fundamentals of evangelism and missions. In football, the fundamentals—block, tackle, pass, and punt—spell out the elation of victory and the agony of defeat. The best team for Christ will be the team that masters the fundamentals.

Obedience Precedes Opportunity

A precondition for mission is obedience. Cleopas and another disciple had an experience with the risen Lord on the road to Emmaus, a village about seven miles from Jerusalem (Luke 24:13). In conversation with the two, our Lord had attempted to explain to the two the meaning of his death and resurrection. Later they returned to Jerusalem and found the eleven and others gathered in a home. They related their experience, and while they were telling what had happened, Jesus appeared among them. When they could not believe that it was actually he, he showed them jagged scars on his hands and feet. He then began explaining to them the meaning of the Scriptures concerning his death and resurrection. He declared that they were to be witnesses of his death, his resurrection, and the repentance-forgiveness relationship of persons with God. He declared that their mission would be to preach and witness to these three essentials of the gospel to all the nations of the earth.

After defining the mission of the church, our Lord tells them, "Behold, I am sending forth the promise of My Father upon you;

but you are to stay in the city until you are clothed with power from on high" (Luke 24:49). He is asking the church to meet the same precondition for mission that he himself met in relation to the Father. He was obedient. Could they afford to wait when the whole world was waiting for the gospel? The most critical factor in our being what God wants us to be is obedience. Now he tests the church by asking it to wait in Jerusalem until it is clothed with power. The command is not to wait until it has studied the situation. The church is not to wait until all the computer printouts are carefully evaluated. He does not tell them to wait until they are sure that they have enough money to finance the projects. Time is never wasted for the church when it is actually waiting upon God for direction.

The opportunity for all the empowering events of Pentecost will not come until Christians are obedient. Our Lord will give to the believer, to the church, and to the denomination the open door of missionary opportunity only when they are obedient to him. Has God set before us an open door of missionary opportunity at this moment in our history? We can answer that by looking at the quality of our obedience to him. The risen Lord has given us direction, but the mission waits on our obedience. If Bold Mission is seen as a denominational promotion, our obedience will be lacking. If we see it as God's imperative, we will be going, growing, and giving. If in our eyes Bold Mission is a denominational theme that changes from year to year, we will probably not give it much weight in our priorities. If it is to us a command of God, we will be able to say, "I was not disobedient to the heavenly vision." Can we actually say at this point that we have been obedient to the heavenly vision he gave us on the Mount of Ascension? Have we obeyed him implicitly in crossing all the frontiers of strangeness to preach the gospel to every person in America? Can we say we have been obedient in the light of a nation that has more Christians per capita than any nation in history and yet that becomes less and less Christian with every passing day?

Are we capable of standing still long enough for him to meet us and empower us for the task of evangelizing this country? Are we capable of keeping silent long enough for him to say to us, "Don't go it alone on this mission." He says, "Wait for the Spirit's power, the Spirit's leadership." We may not be ready to throw off our hang-ups and our traditional ways of doing things to move into a "new Pentecostal age," keeping in step with God who is always making things new. Is there in the Southern Baptist Convention a new desire, a new resolve to obey God without reservation in taking the gospel to every person in the land? How many of our 35,000 pastors and churches are committed to Bold Mission in evangelism and missions? How many of our 85,000 active deacons are ready and willing to obey God as ministers (diakonoi) of Jesus Christ? How many of our more than 200,000 Sunday School teachers are prepared to make every department and every class small groups of committed persons on mission in their marketplace seven days a week?

Obedience precedes opportunity. Whether or not great and effectual doors of evangelistic-missionary opportunity are opened to us will depend on the measure of our obedience. We must be ready to gamble everything on radical obedience to Jesus Christ. Radical love demands radical obedience. It is not a question if we can. We must! For us to be afraid is cowardice. For us to wait is tragic. For us to question is faithless. There is too much at stake for us to fail God. Studdert-Kennedy has put this daring risk of faith in words for us.

> . . . I bet my life on Beauty, Truth,
> And Love, not abstract but incarnate Truth,
> Not Beauty's passing shadow, but its Self.
> It's very self made flesh, Love realized.
> I bet my life on Christ—Christ crucified.[1]

Faith Supersedes Fear

There is a great difference in the attitude of the disciples in the closing chapters of Luke and the Book of Acts. Faith replaced the fear that had gripped their hearts. Peter is a case in point. The lamb becomes the lion. He wavered before the questioning of a little girl during the last hours of Christ's life. Now he stands before the multitude at the Feast of Pentecost, accusing them of crucifying the Son of God. If we listen to our fears, we will never be on Bold Mission. Questions that underline our fears readily come to the forefront when the church decides it will be bold. Can laypersons really be ministers of Christ in the midst of human need? Can we trust laypersons with the gospel? Will our making laypersons responsible for the gospel take away from the dignity and position of ordained clergy? Will supporting laypersons in ministry take monies away from our normal channels of giving? Can we free up church programs to make the necessary changes to transform our churches into lay seminaries to equip laypersons for ministry?

As John Havlik has so well said: "There is a danger in making 'Christ's tigers' out of the domesticated lay pussy cats in the average church." There is risk in every step of faith that the church takes. Since the lay ministry is the ultimate end of the priesthood of the believer, the greatest danger that we face is in failing to equip the laity to do the work of ministry (Eph. 4:11-12). We cannot evangelize and congregationalize America with 35,000 ordained ministers, but we just might be able to do it with 13 million lay ministers. Many of the questions that we raise here ought to be concerns that we face, but never fears that prohibit us from confronting the emergencies of our time. A nation that has assassinated or attempted to assassinate eight of its presidents needs ministry now. A nation that has cities where children are cruelly murdered needs ministry now. These emergency days need emergency measures. We must not let our fears paralyze us into doing nothing while people perish.

Peter might well be the model for the millions of Southern Baptists who admit to failure in their witnessing because of their fears. The experience of Pentecost made a difference in Peter. Fear gave way to faith. Cowardice bowed out for courage. Can we expect our people to become bold witnesses to our faith when thousands of pastors admit to reluctant fears in sharing their faith on a one-to-one basis? Can we even dream of sharing

Christ with every man when we are afraid of the man next door? Can we ever hope to reach every mother, when the mother we know down the street waits on our witness?

A very gracious lady in Mississippi had never witnessed to anyone though she was a fine Christian. She enrolled in a Lay Evangelism School. On Wednesday evening before the field witnessing on Thursday evening she said to the director of the school, "I am frightened but I am not scared." The director asked her what she meant by that. She said, "I am frightened but I will go anyway. If I were scared, I would stay home." We need a lot of Christians who are frightened but not scared.

Jesus, the master Teacher, often taught by demonstration and illustration. When his disciples were fruitless and seemed to be hopeless cases, he had faith in their possibilities. As they walked along a road and talked they passed by a fig tree upon which there was no fruit. He said to the fig tree, "May you never bear fruit again." When they passed that way again the disciples noted that the fig tree had withered and was dying. They called this to the attention of Jesus and he only answered, "Have faith in God."

We ought to fear the danger of a fruitless life much more than we fear bearing our witness. God's answer for fear is faith. He has promised, "I will build my church." That is his part. Witnessing is our part. The Spirit of Christ takes our witness and uses it to bring persons to God. Too often we wait on the results of the computer printout, available monies, or the genius of new leadership. All of that is a cop-out on our doing what God wants us to do now.

> Faith is an affirmation and an act,
> That bids eternal truth be fact.

We strongly affirm the necessity for faith in salvation. We do not as stubbornly insist on faith for mission and ministry. Do we really believe that God has told us to evangelize the world which, when evangelized, God will give to his Christ "the heathen for an inheritance"? Do we really believe that our witness and the mission of the church are related to his second coming? Every man must first hear the gospel (Matt. 24:14). Annie Johnson Flint asks us the question, "What are we doing to bring back the King?"

> Are we doing Thy will? Are we giving Thy message
> to souls Thou hast loved and redeemed on the cross?
> Do we show forth Thy grace to the sad world around us?
> Thy patience in trial, Thy comfort in loss?
> We watch for the signs and we love Thine appearing,
> We long for the peace that Thy kingdom will bring.
> But what are we doing to hasten Thy coming?
> And how are we helping to bring back the King?[2]

Prayer Intercedes Power

Luke says of those who gathered in the upper room to wait for the enduement of power, "And when they had entered, they went up to the upper room, where they were staying; that is, Peter and John and James and Andrew, Philip and Thomas, Bartholomew and Matthew, James the son of Alphaeus, and Simon the Zealot, and Judas the son of James. These all with one mind were continually devoting themselves to prayer, along with the women, and Mary the mother of Jesus, and with His brothers" (Acts 1:13-14). "These . . . were continually devoting themselves to prayer." The power of their Bold Mission was born in bold praying. Prayer may well be the most neglected factor in Southern Baptist Bold Mission.

There is a story that came out of what we call the Middle Ages in Europe. It seems that a simple but very godly monk was touring the Vatican in Rome. The tour guide showed him all the treasures of the Vatican and estimated all the value of these treasures. The guide then said to the monk, "You see my brother, we no longer need to say, 'Silver and gold have we none.' " The monk replied very softly but firmly, "But my brother, can we still say, 'In the name of Jesus, rise up and walk'?" Can it be that with all of our great buildings, our gymnasiums, our day-care centers, our media coverage, we do not have the power of that early church? There may be a lot more activity in the "supper room" than in the "upper room" of our churches. Bold Mission for some of our churches may be the creation of an upper room for those having the gift of intercession. We can talk about 1,200 associations, 35 state conventions, 519 unentered counties, 100 million lost persons, but how many intercessors are there? Black churches in one of their spirituals lament: "He couldn't hear nobody pray."

The power that the witnesses of the New Testament exercised came as a result of prayer. The full significance of the ten days of prayer between the ascension and Pentecost is before us in this chapter. The first cruel blows of persecution could have put the church in full retreat but they found courage and power in prayer. "And when they had prayed, the place where they had gathered together was shaken, and they were all filled with the Holy Spirit, and began to speak the word of God with boldness" (Acts 4:31). This was a case of bold praying for bold mission. Peter and John went to Samaria to investigate the authenticity of the conversions of Samaritans as a result of the preaching of Philip and to pray for them. Prayer not only preceded the mission, it was a part of the mission (8:15 ff.). Cornelius, the non-Christian, and Peter, the Christian, were both praying when the Holy Spirit brought them together (10:2 ff.). Two barriers were crossed as a result of prayer.

When it seemed that the top preacher of the mission was out of service in jail, the church prayed and he was released (12:12). When the church at Antioch saw the need for sending out missionaries the church prayed and the Holy Spirit said to the church, "Set apart for Me Barnabas and Saul for the work to which I have called them" (13:2). Another barrier was crossed as a result of prayer. An outline of Acts is Jerusalem, Judea, Samaria, and the uttermost parts of the earth. Every barrier of class, color, and geography was crossed on the wings of prayer. In all of his epistles the great missionary Paul urges the churches to pray for the mission. He does not urge them to baptize more converts or to beat out all the competition in building a big church. He does urge them to give sacrificially and to pray.

What place does mission and missions have in the prayer life of believers and the church? How many are really praying that the church be found faithful to its missionary obligation? How much of our praying in our prayer meetings is given to meeting our own needs and how much is given to meeting the needs of the world? On Wednesday evening in your church, do church members call the names of lost persons for prayer? In our worship services except for seasonal missionary emphases is there a consciousness of a "partnership in obedience" with the Christians of the world in getting the gospel out to every person? If prayer intercedes power, isn't our prayerlessness the reason for our weakness in evangelism and missions? These are all questions that we must answer for ourselves. God is saying to us as the television commercial for oil filters says, "You can either pay me now or pay me later." Each one of us and each one of our churches will give an account for our stewardship of prayer.

Witness Proceeds Out of Worship

One of the finest illustrations of worship as a preparation for witness is the experience of the young prince Isaiah. When Uzziah, the great king of Israel, lay in state in the palace, the prince came in the magnificent hall of state and saw the body of the king dressed in his royal splendor. The prince quite evidently was thinking about the passing of the king who had brought Israel to a stage of greatness in the world. The king was dead. In contrast to the dead king the young prince saw "the Lord sitting on a throne, lofty and exalted" (Isa. 6:1). The Seraphim called one to another, "Holy, Holy, Holy, is the Lord of Hosts."

Isaiah saw himself as mortal and sinful, and he confessed his mortality and his sinfulness. In a great religious experience he felt cleansed by his confession of sin. Then he heard the voice of the missionary God telling him that he had been cleansed and asking, "Whom shall I send, and who will go for us?" Isaiah replied, "Here am I, send me." God sent him on mission that seemed hopeless. God sent him to a people who would listen but not understand. Their hearts would be insensible; their eyes would not see; their ears would not hear, but Isaiah must go anyway. When Isaiah asked how long he would have to do this, God answered: "Until the cities are destroyed, until houses are without inhabitants, and the land is utterly desolate" (see Isa. 6:9-11).

It will take more than the energies of the flesh to turn our pastors into burning evangelists and earnest equippers of the saints. It will take more than passing resolutions to motivate, train, and equip laypersons for ministry. It will take more than "gritting our teeth and getting with it" to plant churches within the reach of every person. It will take more than denominational oratory or programs to give every person the opportunity to hear and respond to the gospel. It will take a worship experience like Isaiah's in the palace of Uzziah or that of Moses by the burning bush or that of Gideon beneath the oak tree at Ophrah to send us out in faithful witness to our Lord.

We need a worship experience where we will tremble again before his almightiness and power, where we will stand in awe of our mortality and his unchanging person and purpose, where we will hear again his word of promise and commission; and where we will feel again the compulsion of his love; and we will see our lives in the light of his revelation of himself in the face of Jesus Christ. No great person in Christian history has ever been able to rise to greatness without a great worship experience in which that person was able to see the Lord high and lifted up. In such experience we see our sinfulness. In cleansing we have finally come to the place where God can share his mission with us by asking, "Who will go for us?" Then we have the privilege of great commitment: "Here am I, send me."

There is a word that we have to say to each other before we can say that saving word to the world. We have to call each other back to the basics of evangelistic and missionary zeal. Obedience, faith, prayer, and worship are the fundamentals. Let us walk beyond the trivialities. Eliminate all personal pettiness. Turn up the lights. Hang out the signs. Ring all the bells. The church is awake because he is alive. Spell out from the Word of God the dynamics that equip the hearts and minds of the believers for the challenges of the marketplaces, the homes, and the highways in the traffic patterns of their daily lives. Speak of the grace that creates new energies of faith that flourish under the stress of both success and failure. Speak of the hope that spells help for humanity, hurt and wounded by life. Speak of the love that will make us compassionate with people, bad as they are, and good as they can be without God's help.

There is a word we have to say to the world when we have come from the hills of obedience, faith, prayer, and worship. We will say to the world, "No, thank you, we refuse to join you in your racial, religious, or class pride, or your scorn for people. We do not withdraw or flee from you. We stand in solidarity with you as humans. We share your agony and your ecstasy of living. We are among you to help, to care, to bear, and to share. We are looking and indeed we believe we have found what you are looking for—the losing that is finding and the dying that is living. We are not pretending to be your savior or your judge, we only know him who is both Savior and Judge. We fellowship with One who is with us to forgive and serve. We believe that we can look and find together the power to free us from the treadmill of anxiety and the love that rescues the fallen from futility." That, dear hearts, is Bold Mission.

Notes

1. *The Best of G. A. Studdert-Kennedy* (New York: Harper and Brothers, 1924, 1927, 1929, 1948), p. 49.
2. Flint, *Poems*, Vol. 2.

7

A Clear Call to Commitment

Timothy was Paul's protégé, best-loved disciple, and closest friend. It is not often that a man can be all of this to another man. Their relationship was framed in very personal family experiences, forged in the fires of adversity, and full of mutual admiration. Only Timothy is mentioned in the letters of Paul from all four periods of his writing. Timothy means "honored by God" or "honoring God." The name was given to him by his Christian grandmother Lois and Christian mother Eunice. His father was a Greek and may not have been a Christian. They lived in Derbe or Lystra and it was there that Paul on his first missionary journey brought the young man to a saving knowledge of Jesus Christ (Acts 14:6-7). On his second missionary journey Paul visited the family again and Timothy was circumcised, ordained, and joined Paul on his second mission (16:1-3; 1 Tim. 4:14; 2 Tim. 1:6). Timothy was one of the spiritual compensations Paul received for his cruel treatment in Lystra.

Paul had such confidence in the young man that he delegated to him very difficult tasks in Thessalonica, Corinth, and Ephesus (1 Thess. 3:1-2; 1 Cor. 4:17; 16:10; 1 Tim. 4:14-16; 5:20-23; 6:11-14,20; 2 Tim. 1:14; 2:1-7; 4:1-2). Paul tells the Philippians that Timothy is the only one he can send to them because he does not think about himself but about others (Phil. 2:19-21). When Paul knew he did not have long to live, he wanted Timothy to be with him (2 Tim. 4:9). To this young man perhaps about thirty years of age in AD 67, Paul writes two of his letters that have come to us in the Holy Scriptures.

Men are great not because they have no weaknesses but because they rise to greatness in spite of their weaknesses. There is ample evidence that Timothy had two weaknesses and for one of these he was not responsible. He was naturally timid and physically weak (1 Cor. 4:17; 16:10-11; 1 Tim. 4:14-16; 5:20-23; 6:11-14,20; 2 Tim. 1:14; 2:1-7; 4:1-2). Timothy is evidence that neither physical weakness nor natural timidity need keep us from being strong and bold. Paul and Timothy both served the God who is able to make our weakness into strength and our timidity into courage. Strength and courage are born when weakness and timidity are renounced and forsaken. No one knew this any better than Paul who said, "He has said to me, 'My grace is sufficient for you, for power is perfected in weakness.' Most gladly, therefore, I will rather boast about my weaknesses, that the power of Christ may dwell in me" (2 Cor. 12:9).

The news of the imprisonment of the great spiritual freedom fighter of the Christian faith must have been devastating for Timothy and for all the Christians. There was a feeling that this was it for the apostle born out of season. He was not in his hired house so the letter must have come from the Tullanium as notorious in its day as was Laforce in *The Tale of Two Cities* by Charles Dickens. So many prisoners had been eaten alive by rats in the Tullanium that it was known as The Sepulchre. The sentence of death hung over the apostle. The dark cloud of persecution that was over him was not as dark as the cloud of fear that hung over the Christian community from Rome to Jerusalem.

Many clear calls to commitment have the odor of prison damp about them. The Epistle to the Philippians, Dietrich Bonhoeffer's *Prison Epistles*, John Bunyan's *The Pilgrim's Progress*, and Paul's second letter to Timothy all came from dark, damp, and fetid prison cells. Some men sit and curse the darkness, and others light a candle in the dark. Some men look through prison bars and see the mud. Others look through prison bars and see the stars. Paul looked up and penned an epistle to his son in the ministry that gained immortality in the Holy Scriptures.

A poignant passage from the second letter to Timothy underlines the apostle's privations in the Tullanium. "When you come bring the cloak which I left at Troas with Carpus, and the books, especially the parchments . . . Make every effort to come before winter" (2 Tim. 4:13,21a). He is asking Timothy to bring him everything he owned. Persons can be measured by what they hold dear. Paul needs a friend. He needs the Scriptures. He needs books. He needs a cloak. These are the treasures that are really worthwhile. A cloak to warm his body and a friend to warm his spirit. Books to fire his intellect and Scriptures to fire his soul. Timothy is urged to bring these things before the winter that Paul may never see. Another great God lover, William Tyndale, wrote a similar word from his damp prison cell at Vilvorde that takes its place with Paul's in immortality.

I entreat your lordship, and that by the Lord Jesus, that if I must remain here for the winter, you would beg the Commissary to be so kind as to send me, from the things of mine which he has, a warmer cap—I feel the cold painfully in my head. Also a warmer cloak to patch my leggings. My overcoat is worn out, my shirts even are worn out. He has a woolen shirt of mine, if he will send it. But most of all I entreat and implore your kindness to do your best with the Commissary to be so good as to send me my Hebrew Bible, grammar and vocabulary, that I may spend time in that pursuit.

Prerequisites to Commitment

Phygelus and Hermogenes have already deserted Paul and now he is writing to his young co-worker who is filled with timidity and fear. Against the dark background of the desertion of two co-workers and the timidity and fear of another, Paul flings the flaming torch of Christian commitment. In 2 Timothy 1:7, Paul reminds Timothy of some prerequisites for Christian commitment. God has not given us a timid or fearful spirit, but a spirit of power, of love, and a sound mind. He reminds Timothy of those inner resources that every believer has available. Another word for power is ability. To the early church waiting in Jerusalem, fearing that the sword of persecution would soon descend upon all of them, the risen Lord says, "You shall receive power when the Holy Spirit has come upon you; and you shall be My witnesses" (Acts 1:8). That enabling work of grace helped them

to face privation, whippings, imprisonment, and death with boldness and courage that impressed even their enemies. Very few
believers in our country are facing that kind of opposition, but we
need ability to overcome our indifference, our complacency, and
our surrender to culture.

The greatest of all spiritual gifts is love. "There is no fear in
love; but perfect love casts out fear" (1 John 4:18). The demon
of fear is exorcised by love. For the fearful young pastor, Paul
prescribes love. When we love people who are without Christ,
we will not need a "how to" manual to get rid of our fears of witnessing to them. Love reaches out to others. When Bramwell
Booth told the general that he was blind, the general sought to
comfort him, and Bramwell said, "There is no fear, only love
driving me on and on." The last of this triad of Christian blessings
is a sound mind. Paul is talking about a healthy, fearless view of
our circumstances. Those who are older remind us of the time
that our whole nation was gripped with fear and one man crip-
pled with polio calmed a whole nation by reminding them that,
"We have nothing to fear except fear itself." Most of our fears of
a real Christian commitment "to the death" are unreasoned
fears. The Christian above all others should possess the ability to
see things clearly. The best translation of the first phrase of Philippians 1:10 is, "that you may be able to test the things that
make a difference." There is no substitute for a sound mind.

Timothy, "Fan the flame of faith in your own heart, and remember that that faith was given you by your mother Eunice and
your grandmother Lois" (2 Tim. 1:5-6, author's translation). It is
easy for the flame of faith in our hearts to die down. With many
of us it may be only a small burning ember. Paul urges Timothy
as a prerequisite to commitment to fan the dying embers into a
flame. One of the things that will help us to fan the flame is to
remember those who have gone before us. It helps us to remember the broad shoulders that have carried us to this day. Ben C.
Fisher, the retired executive director of the Education Commission of the Southern Baptist Convention, tells about the doctor
informing him that he had a deep-seated malignancy and that he

had only a few months or years to live. Soon after he was given this news he relates an experience in revisiting the old home place.

In recent months I had occasion to visit the little mountain cemetery where for two hundred years my people have been laid to rest. On the slightly leaning and lichen-covered stone of my great-great grandfather I saw these words: "These are they that came out of great tribulation, and are washed in the blood of the lamb."

As we walked slowly on that beautiful spring day down the mountain toward the old church, I reflected on the values and commitments of these departed saints. They believed they were accountable to God both in life and eternity. They believed in His word, kept His commandments, had reverence for His house, loved their neighbor, and died in faith.

Down near the foot of the mountain I noticed an inscription which I had never seen before, but which sums up all I have been trying to say about the ultimate future and the presence of hope:

"The Shepherd will come for His sheep,
And the valley will bloom again."[1]

In Dostoyevsky's novel, *The Brothers Karamazov,* the prosecuting attorney says of Dimitri, "He is always ready to espouse any cause, providing it costs him nothing." Paul tells Timothy that he must not be ashamed of his faith or his friend, and that it will cost him everything (2 Tim. 1:8). It would have been easy for Timothy to say what some Christians were saying. "If Paul is so right and so committed, why does God allow him to be in jail?" "Paul is OK I guess, but why does he have to be so radical?" "It's all right to be Christian but you don't have to go around trying to convince everyone." Boldness and the ability to lose oneself in a cause are requisites to commitment. Paul's final word to Timothy in chapter 1 is: "Seize the sound words that I have taught you and never let go" (see 2 Tim. 1:13). Old paths are not necessarily right paths, but one does well to consider where the fathers have walked. It is not accidental that our great highway systems follow very often the paths of the pioneers who followed the Indian trails, who followed the game trails. There is a particular set to the jaw that spells determination in Paul's words, "and never let go."

The Nature of Commitment

To his weak and timid son in the gospel, Paul sends a clear call to commitment. "You, therefore, my child, strengthen yourself in the grace which is in Christ Jesus, and the things which you have heard from me supported by many witnesses, pass on to the responsibility of faithful persons competent to teach others. Take your share in suffering hardship as a true soldier of Jesus Christ" (2 Tim. 2:1-3, author's translation). I have emphasized the Greek middle voice in verse 1 to read, "Strengthen yourself." This is something that not even God or the great apostle can do for Timothy.

When fair-weather disciples are deserting the cause, the leader of the cause says, "Strengthen yourself." When the leader faces death in the Tullanium and the disciples everywhere are facing persecution and death, the leader says, "Strengthen yourself." In a time of crisis and portent for the kingdom, David says to Solomon, "Be strong." In a national crisis caused by backsliding, Azariah says to Asa, king of Judah, "Be strong." In a time of testing for the people of God ridden with fear, Isaiah says to all the fearful, "Be strong." Paul, writing to the Corinthian church beset by moral weakness in the midst of a city of lust and luxury urges them to "Be strong." One of the major ingredients of commitment is strength of character.

In verse 3 I have omitted "therefore" which evidence indicates is not in the best Greek texts. I have added the fact of participation in the suffering which is correctly translated in 1:8 as "Be a partaker of the suffering of the gospel." It should be present in verse 3 as well. Again this is something that no one else can do for Timothy. It involves an act of the will. "Take your share of the suffering." What Paul is talking about is commitment. "Strengthen yourself." "Take your share of the suffering." The Christian faith is not for Monday-morning quarterbacks and drawing-room fullbacks. There is a call to get in the game. John Drinkwater's poetry says it well.

Grant us the will to fashion as we feel,
Grant us the strength to labour as we know,
Grant us the purpose ribbed and edged with steel,
To strike the blow.

Knowledge we ask not; knowledge Thou hast sent;
But Lord, the will—there lies our deepest need.
Grant us to build above the deep intent,
The deed, the deed.

Commitment leaves us with no options. In earlier days of jet travel when the *Boeing 707* was new, I boarded one that was equipped to handle some of the military emergencies of those days. I had watched ground crews load a freight section occupying one half of the cabin space with military supplies. Then I saw a contingent of infantry march into what would have been the tourist space, each man carrying full infantry packs. The agent then informed the few civilian passengers that we would all be in the first-class cabin. All this time I had been looking at the runway that terminated at the foot of a mountain range. We lumbered out to the runway and took our position, facing the mountains. I was thinking about that enormous load. The crew got their clearance and the captain called for takeoff power. We began our run for takeoff, and I was thinking about the load and the mountains. I knew there was a line on that runway and once we reached it all options were gone. It was either takeoff or crash. It is the line of commitment. That is commitment. All options are gone. There is no turning back. I think that is what Jesus meant when he said, "No one, after putting his hand to the plow and looking back, is fit for the kingdom of God" (Luke 9:62).

Timothy is in Christ and Christ is in Timothy. No one has yet probed the deepest meanings of the mystery of the union between Christ and the believer. The one singular reality we must face is that we are in Christ. So Paul says, "Strengthen yourself in that reality." Grace is Christ in presence and action. Grace is inseparable from Christ. This becomes our talisman, our daystar, our orientation for all of life. We are in Christ, in grace. The new orientation that becomes ours when we are in Christ is not automatic. It doesn't just happen. We are to strengthen ourselves in it.

Paul tells Timothy that there is no way of escaping the hard words of the Christian faith. God has never promised us a rose garden. In the Christian faith there is no way of going to heaven "on flowery beds of ease." Our hymn is, "Sure I must fight if I would reign, increase my courage Lord." One cannot soften the hard demands of words like love and live, go and give, or suffer and sacrifice. These are words that are as red as blood and as hard as nails. They cannot be avoided or evaded by the committed Christian. God cannot do for us as pastors, churches, deacons, Sunday School teachers, and denominational leaders what only we can do for ourselves. As an act of the will we must strengthen ourselves in the grace that is in Christ Jesus and take our share of suffering hardship. There is a need for us to pray with Christina Rossetti:

> God harden me against myself,
> This coward with pathetic voice
> Who craves for rest, and ease, and joys;
> Myself, archtraitor to myself,
> My hollowest friend, my deadliest foe,
> My clog whatever road I go.
> Yet one there is can curb myself,
> Can roll the strangling load from me,
> Break off the yoke and set me free.

During the Nazi occupation of Norway, the bishop of Norway sent a pastoral letter to be read in every church. The letter was a ringing call to commitment to the congregations of the church of Norway. The pastoral letter which was read in every church sometimes with Nazi spies present began with the words, "There is a foe. There is a fight. There is a faith." From our text there comes a clear call to commitment. Our text says: There is a faith . . . There is a fight . . . There is a fellowship.

Commitment to a Faith

There is such a thing as "faith of our Fathers living still, in spite of dungeon, fire, and sword." Paul reminds Timothy that the gift of God which is in him is the living faith of his mother and grand-mother. A faith that has no sense of history makes no sense at all. Jude, the slave of Jesus Christ, writes to all loved by the father and kept in Jesus Christ and says, "I felt the necessity to write to you appealing that you contend earnestly for the faith which was once for all delivered to the saints" (Jude 3). There is a great cloud of witnesses who challenge us to a commitment to our faith. "Therefore, since we have so great a cloud of witnesses surrounding us, let us also lay aside every encumbrance, and the sin which so easily entangles us, and let us run with endurance the race that is set before us" (Heb. 12:1).

Our faith is the faith of those known and unknown Old and New Testament heroes of the faith. They subdued kingdoms, wrought righteousness, stopped the mouths of lions, quenched the violence of fire, turned to flight the armies of the aliens, suf-fered trials of scourging and mockings, wandered about clothed in the skins of animals, and lived in dens and caves of the earth. All the while they were testifying that they were only pilgrims in this world because they had a higher citizenship and a better country as their goal and glory.

Our faith is the faith of Balthasar Hübmaier whose lay preachers in a single year brought to him 12,000 converts for baptism. His lay preachers had a life expectancy of only three years once they espoused the faith. It is the faith of the first Bap-tists who were driven from country to country, persecuted for their faith, and driven from their home. They came to this land of liberty and found persecution here as well. They persevered in the faith and lived to influence the making of our republic and to become the largest group of evangelicals in the new world. It is the faith of Daniel Marshall and Shubal Stearns, our fathers in the faith. Their faith was fanned into flame in the Great Awaken-ing. Driven from Virginia, they founded the Sandy Creek Church in Guilford County, North Carolina, and that church established mission churches from Chesapeake Bay to Georgia and from the Atlantic to the Kentucky frontier. It is the faith of the Bagbys who suffered stoning and ridicule to preach the faith in

Brazil's great growing cities. It is the faith of Carroll who established a seminary on the plains of Texas during the fire and fervor of the Awakening of 1890-1920.

Our faith is quite certainly the faith of those modern pioneers of home missions who saw Southern Baptist churches, associations, and state conventions where there were none and by faith wrote new chapters in missionary sacrifice. These pioneers of home missions never went to some strange foreign land, but in terms of sacrifice and commitment no one has ever written a more beautiful story of missionary zeal and courage. There are names like Lawrence, Redford, Brantley, Cash, and many others whose faith to evangelize this nation was unwavering and shining like the stars. All of these adventurers are not dead. They still witness, plant churches, organize associations, form state conventions. They are committed. They know how to sing the Lord's song in a strange land. They are not looking back to the place they came from. That is why God is so proud of them.

What is the state of our commitment to our faith in the presence of these witnesses? Is our faith a faith that flickers rather than flames? Is it a faith that hesitates rather than undertakes? Is it a faith that compromises rather than conquers? A free translation of 2 Timothy 1:14 is: "Hold the great securities of your faith intact by the help of the Holy Spirit." There are some things about which the church or the believer cannot hesitate or stutter. A good discipline for some of our present insecurities about things that we need to be sure of would be an earnest study of the writings of E. Y. Mullins and B. H. Carroll along with our Bibles. Another good discipline would be a constant reminder to ourselves that the faith must not be just affirmed, it must be lived. The latter takes a bit more doing than the former.

We must keep intact our faith in Christ. "Jesus Christ is Lord" must be more than an article of faith. It must become an act of personal commitment to his lordship. It will demand a very close look at our likeness to him. As leaders of our lives and our churches, our commitment to him must be more than a statement about the fact that he is Leader. We must follow him to the ends of the earth and to the end of time. There must be an insistence that our willingness to follow him is on his priority and not ours. The fact that he is Number One in our lives must be more than an uplifted finger for number one. We will have to understand that his being Number One will mean our fleshing out such words as, "Blessed are the pure in heart for they shall see God," and "Blessed are the peacemakers, for they shall be called the children of God," and "You shall love the Lord your God, with all your heart, and with all your soul, and with all your strength, and with all your mind; and your neighbor as yourself."

We must keep intact our faith in the gospel. It is our stubborn conviction that there is nothing wrong with man that the gospel cannot address and redeem. His moral purity is the answer to all world religions. Other religions have a body of teaching but they do not have a gospel, because they do not have Christ. His impeccable moral purity is our answer to all would-be saviors, cultists, and false messiahs. His atoning death is the answer for all the world's alienation and sin. For all the brokenness of society that pits class against class, color against color, and nation against nation, that atoning death breaks down the wall of partition and makes both one. His miraculous resurrection is the answer to all of our questions about life and death and heaven and hell. He alone "breaks the power of cancelled sin and sets the prisoner free." His coming again in majesty and power is the answer to the world's alienation and the threat of nuclear hell. We are not "ashamed of the gospel, for it is the power of God for salvation" (Rom. 1:16).

We must keep intact our faith in one another, our churches, and our denomination. Even though we are aware of moral lapse or a heretical doctrinal position, we still need a faith in one another as believers. Constant suspicion of one another is fatal to our cause and divides the body of Christ, crucifying Christ again. We must never draw a circle around ourselves and what we believe so tightly that it becomes smaller and smaller and eventually we find ourselves alone.

Commitment to a Fight

There is a foe and there is a fight. If our Christian experience involves no struggle, we are not like Christ, and we are not like the Christians of the first century, and we are not like the greatest Christians of all history. Paul used military terminology quite often to call the freedom-faith fighters into the struggle.

Finally, be strong in the Lord, and in the strength of His might. Put on the full armor of God, that you may be able to stand firm against the schemes of the devil. For our struggle is not against flesh and blood, but against the rulers, against the powers, against the world forces of this darkness, against the spiritual forces of wickedness in the heavenly places. Therefore, take up the full armor of God, that you may be able to resist in the evil day, and having done everything, to stand firm. Stand firm therefore" (Eph. 6:10-14).

Often we do a better job of singing about the struggle than we do getting into it. The hymns and songs of our faith are full of allusions to the struggle and our involvement in it. We sing:

Sure I must fight, if I would reign,
Increase my courage, Lord;
I'll bear the toil, endure the pain,
Supported by Thy word.

or we sing

At the sign of triumph Satan's host doth flee:
On then Christian soldiers, on to victory!
Hell's foundations quiver at the shout of praise!
Brothers lift your voices, loud your anthems raise.

or we sing,

Lead on, O king eternal, The day of march has come;
Henceforth in fields of conquest Thy tents shall be our home:
Thro' days of preparation Thy grace has made us strong,
And now, O King eternal, We lift our battle song.

The New Testament talks about our struggle with the world, the flesh, and the devil. It speaks of the three dimensions of sin. The "devil" is sin above us—cosmic evil. The "world" is sin around us—social evil. The "flesh" is sin within us—personal evil. All three are realities and all three must be struggled against. Generally, evangelical Christians have been able to see evil within and they quite readily speak out against personal sins such as adultery, drunkenness, and violent crime. Those same Christians quite often have difficulty seeing the evil in society and in seeing evil in its cosmic dimension. Evil that is long entrenched in society and that has become a part of our culture is much more difficult to resist and to speak out against.

The struggle against sin within ourselves often falls under the delusions of the devil. We come to see personal sin in terms of adultery, drunkenness, and violence against another and not in terms of the neglect of love, mercy, and justice. Jesus pointed this out to the Pharisees on several occasions. They thought about sin in terms of failure to tithe and not in terms of the lack of a Christian attitude toward others. The evil temper, the racial prejudice, the liar, and the thief within all of us require us to be strong in the grace that is in Christ Jesus. We may have observed the church leader who fought immorality in others falling prey to it. "Sweep your own doorstep" is more than a good adage. It is very close to what Jesus talked about many times.

The struggle against evil in society is difficult because it often becomes political. Politics is not a bad word. Anything that involves people is political. There are many good church people who may never commit great sins, but because of their position or their influence they become a part of an unjust or corrupt system that sins against the rights of people. They may be a part of a system that tolerates and even encourages poverty. We must do more than minister to the victims of the world's injustices, we must cry out against them in the tradition of the Hebrew prophets and Jesus of Nazareth. Backing out of inflation caused by government spending sprees, money-hungry corporations, and market manipulators on the backs of the poor and the needy is not just.

See the social evil in the face of the "bag woman," her face pressed against the glass of Rich's display window. She is looking at the toys and remembering happier days when there was a husband and children. Now everything she owns is in that battered shopping bag. Tonight she will sleep in a furnace room just off a downtown street. She will sleep there because of a friendly custodian who will leave the door open for her. See the evil in the love-hungry, vivid in the face of a battered child trying to kiss the brute who beat her. Hear her saying, "Daddy, I love you," to the sick unfeeling monster whose face is filled with anger, animosity, and frustration. See the evil in the raucous calls of the teenage prostitute. Six months ago she was a teenager going to Sunday School in Vienna, Georgia. See the evil in the young couple defeated in their struggle against a credit-card culture and the "social drink" society. They are breaking up their marriage, scarring for life a kid who never asked to be born.

We must do more than see the evil. We must resist it. We must fight against it. We must challenge Pharaoh in his corporate and governmental offices to let the people go. An important part of this struggle is our ministry to persons who have been bruised and battered by life. The Christian Life Commission of the Southern Baptist Convention and the Social Ministries Department of the Home Mission Board have tried to be a conscience for our denomination in this struggle against "rulers" and "powers." There is a great deal of resistance to getting involved in ministry. Often it is unsung and unrewarded. That was true of the ministry of our Lord. His resistance to evil in society and his befriending of the poor and the rejected finally nailed him to a cross. The church like our Lord must touch the festering sores of society.

Evil in its cosmic proportions must be resisted and prayed against. There are times when man seems to lose control, and demonic powers over which man has no power take over. There was such a time when the beast of Berlin took over and led the world into holocaust. There are times when man reaches the end of mind, and the end of mind is madness. Only a demonic mind and demonic plan could include the rape and murder of Cambodia and nuclear war. Part of our plan for Bold Mission might be a call for world Christians to begin a concert of prayer against those who would destroy humanity and erase the last vestiges of the Creator in the creation. The struggle is not just against flesh and blood. There is a foe and there is a fight.

Commitment to a Fellowship

One cannot eliminate the concept of participation from verse 8. When Paul calls upon Timothy to take his full share of suffering, he is talking about the same thing that he desired for himself when he told the Philippians that he wants to know Christ "in the fellowship of his suffering." H. H. Farmer, in a series of lectures at Southern Seminary years ago, said that "the American church has every mark of the New Testament church except the mark of suffering." It is not just that we have escaped persecution. We have brought the "happiness cult" into the church. Christians are supposed to wear a perennial smile. What Farmer was talking about was our failure to enter into the mystery of his suffering. In some Christian groups in the South Pacific they practice "holy weeping." It is a mystical sharing of the sufferings of Christ. Not many American Christians have read or can even appreciate such classics as Tholuck's *Light from the Cross.*

Taking our share of the suffering means that we know, understand, and feel the weight, the woe, and the worry of the world's sin and suffering. We will feel like Booth, the founder of the Salvation Army, who after walking the streets of London one night came home and awakened his wife. He said to sleepy Catherine, "Catherine, wake up and pray with me. I have felt the fires of hell. All London is going to hell tonight." One hears Christians say, "I don't feel the guilt of racism. I don't feel guilty for what my fathers did to the slaves." Is it because we have never had our Gethsemane? We have never said, "Father, if there is any way let this cup pass away, but if it must be, it must be. I want to do your will." To take our share of the suffering means that we will feel the shame of the prostitute, the guilt of the thief, the rejection of the battered child, the emptiness of the abandoned wife, the loneliness of the aged couple, and the self-disgust of the alcoholic.

Taking our share of the suffering will mean that we will be committed to bold witnessing even though our motives will be misinterpreted, our methods will be questioned, and our message will be disbelieved. It will mean that we will like being like the Man for others. His mission will take priority because it is a mission for others. Missions overseas will not be a substitute for missions in our own backyard. Buildings and programs for our self-preservation will not take the place of his mission to the lost, neglected, and rejected of our community and the world. We will not be happy about our overloaded tables and bursting garbage cans while most of the world goes hungry. Our expensive and wasteful life-styles will become distasteful in light of the simplicity of his life and the desperation of the world's millions. We will begin to understand the scenario of the Christian life-style—the way up is down—the way to get is give—the way to live is die— the way to forgiveness is forgiving—the way to being loved is loving—the way to eternal life is dying to self. This scenario of paradox is his way for us and for the church.

Commitment is an act of the will. That is the reason Paul cannot do for Timothy what even God cannot do for him. It will take an act of the will for Timothy to "strengthen himself in the grace that is in Christ Jesus," and to "take his full share of the suffering as a true soldier of Jesus Christ." I can tell and write about the need. I can tell and write about the fair-weather disciples that are constantly deserting him. I can tell and write about the faith of our fathers and their heroic lives and sacrifices, *but I cannot make a commitment for you.* That is something only I can do for myself and only you can do for yourself. You can do it now as you read the final words of this chapter. He is with you now as you read, just as he is with me now as I write. He is waiting on us and our full commitment to him and to his mission to the ends of the earth and to the end of time.

Note

1. Paper, "The Ultimate Future and the Presence of Hope," prepared for the Education Commission Conference on Missions, 1979.

8
Love, the Heartbeat of Home Missions

In one episode of *Logan's Run*, a science fiction television show that had its demise several years ago, Logan, Jessica, and the android Rem are closing in on Sanctuary. They are on the run, fleeing the Domed City which is the epitome of the demonic. The Domed City is a loveless world of computers, robots, and dehumanized people. The nuclear war of the twenty-second century destroyed civilization except for the Domed City and a group of people who became primitives living in ignorance. Logan and Jessica, having discovered love, are fleeing the hell of manipulated people living in a society where birth and death, thought and speech, sex and marriage are all preplanned for every one by the Allwise Ones.

Sanctuary is a legend that really exists somewhere in the place where the primitives live. The legend is that there one can find meaning and love. The secret is there. Sanctuary is more than a legend. It is a giant computer console in which all the accumulated history and knowledge of the human race is stored. More important, in it are recorded all the mistakes of humanity and their failure to love which ended in nuclear war that destroyed all the persons that stored the knowledge.

The three science fiction refugees discover the great computer console. The primitives think it is an altar and they worship there. They threaten with death anyone who touches it. All they need to do is press one button activating it and all the knowledge of mankind is theirs. They stand before it genuflecting and mumbling litanies of worship but never open its secrets. All they need to do is just press one button that activates the voice and the screen. The computer would print out for them all they needed to know to build a perfect society based on love.

Today when we look at our nation we see on one hand a plastic society lost in materialism, secularism, and scientism. They are the zombies of the world that they have molded with their own hands. Anything is right that is right for you. The Almighty Plastics are in charge—MasterCard, VISA, and American Express. You do not save money for there is nothing to save for. Children are a drag so you don't produce any. Marriage is hopeless so you don't indulge. Church and biblical morality are endangered species, just leftovers from a lower evolutionary stage. This society is best at producing floods of pornography and movies featuring sex kittens, psychos, and ax murderers. Anything that will tickle the ends of jaded nerves is eagerly sought and consumed. Lots of downers to sleep and lots of uppers to wake up are indispensable to the zombies who mistake conviviality for love, sex for happiness, and money for success. The battered child, domestic murders, and psychological killers are recurring nightmares that haunt the daily news. Fear stalks our streets and invades our sleep.

In the midst of all this there is a revival of mindless religion dedicated to religious ignorance, superstition, and oppression. Cultic leaders claim the bodies and souls of mindless devotees. Attempting to satisfy an inner hunger, millions worship at the altar of the bizarre and the exotic. Held in bondage by superstitious fears and hopes, they are ignorant of all true principles of religion and of everything that speaks clearly about God and human destiny. All those upon whom the lovelight of Calvary has shined cannot help but feel powerful pathos for those who are enslaved to ignorant dread, blind hope, misguided priests, and religious charlatans.

The consequence of this is that we have at one and the same time religion and irreligion that appeal to the highest heaven for reproof, correction, and guidance. In the midst of all this the church of Jesus Christ has the power to release the one saving Word of God. In our churches the missionary message of the Bible within the Book on the altar or on the pulpit is carefully dusted and verbally affirmed, but very often ignored, and the world of irreligion and perversion of religion waits in vain for the missionary that never comes and the message that is never heard. Like the primitives in our science fiction episode we worship the book but never release the potential of its power in the loveless world which has never discovered that "God is love."

The message that God is working to produce a new society in which there is neither Jew nor Gentile, a society of love, is saved for the sanctuary and not shared with the world. When more than 85 million people in our country are still unevangelized, can we say that we are really hearing, believing, and transmitting the message of the redeeming love of God? Are we really sharing the message of that sanctuary in the "Rock of Ages" or like the primitives in *Logan's Run* are we just repeating slick phrases about it to one another? The missionary task is more than affirming a passing interest in missions. It is more than a momentary feeling of pity generated by some heartrending tale of human need or instance of cruel suffering. It is more than a human conception born in the heart of some great missionary who gave his life for others. William Owen Carver has defined missions as "the extensive realization of God's redemptive purpose in Christ by means of human messengers."[1]

The missionary task of the church is to take the good news where it is news. One is never a missionary or ever won to Christ by the missionary message until the gospel is news. The missionary is one who is constantly overwhelmed by the "newness" of the gospel. When the gospel becomes old hat to the pastor, the church, or the denomination, they cease to be missionary. When persons never get over the newsiness of the gospel, they are missionaries. "God is love" is news. "God so loved the world" is news. "Christ loved us and gave himself for us" is news. "God is actually making his appeal through us" is news. The heartbeat of home missions is the love of God. The gospel of John and his epistles focus for us on the love of God.

> For God so loved the world, that He gave His only begotten Son, that whoever believes in Him should not perish, but have eternal life.
> The one who does not love does not know God, for God is love. By this the love of God was manifested in us, that God has sent His only begotten Son into the world so that we might live through Him. In this is love, not that we loved God, but that He loved us and sent His Son to be the propitiation for our sins.
> We know love by this, that He laid down His life for us; and we ought to lay down our lives for the brethren (John 3:16; 1 John 4:8-10; 3:16).

I want to paraphrase what these passages say and add what Paul says to us in 2 Corinthians 5:19-20.

> God cared so much about the world that he shared with us his only Son Jesus the Christ so that everyone who puts trust in him as Savior and Lord will not end up in hell but will have eternal life. The person who does not care about God and others does not know God because God is caring. God has shown us his caring in Jesus and in persons who have trusted Jesus so we might have his life in us. We did not care about God first. He cared about us before we cared about him. He shared his love for us long ago by sharing his Son who bore our sins. We know that his caring is in us because we are like him. We want to give our lives for others who do not know him. In this way we all are missionaries for Jesus Christ because we are actually making God's appeal to persons who are not Christians.

The Nature of Love

In order to communicate with the pagan mind in a sex-soaked culture such as ours, we need a word for love that gives new meaning to the one word that is at the heart of the Christian message. In America today we love apple pie, mother, automobiles, hairstyles, and people. Our language is impoverished at this point. In the above very free paraphrase of biblical statements we have substituted the word *caring* for love. Love is caring, sharing, and bearing. These are the three words that stand out in our paraphrase. It is difficult for us to share the God kind of love *(agape)* with a culture that knows nothing about it. Paul said that love is the greatest of all the Christian gifts and pointed out the true nature of God kind of love. "Love . . . does not seek its own

. . . love is patient, love is kind, and is not jealous . . . bears all things, believes all things, hopes all things, endures all things (1 Cor. 13:4-7). Paul is saying in another way that love is caring, sharing, and bearing.

"God cared so much about the world." Another way to say this is that "God was so concerned about the world." I care means that I am emotionally involved. Are we emotionally involved with the more than 85 million persons in the United States who are without Christ? Are we emotionally involved with that one person in our community who is without Christ? Can we turn the full light of this missionary text on the spiritual needs of the millions and the one? Do we care that hundreds of girls sell themselves to a pimp for prostitution? Do we care that some of our neighbors are unemployed and their children may go hungry? Do we care about that busy businessman who is so intent on climbing the ladder of corporate success that he has forgotten God? Do we care that our churches are sharing so little of their resources for the world mission of the church? Do we care about the hungry children of the world who are becoming nothing but skin, bones, and swollen bellies? Do we care about the alcoholics, drug addicts, and teenage criminals in our own city?

Love is sharing. One of the youth songs asks two questions that are both pointed and poignant: "Do you really care? Do you care enough to share?" What is the level of your caring? The possessive drive is very strong in human nature. Two children quarreling in the street over a toy and two adults who agreed to share in marriage quarreling over what belongs to whom are commentaries on our obesession with possession. But love cuts across nature as Paul Tillich points out in *Love, Power and Justice*. The love of God cuts into all earthly and natural "loves" as *agape*. The nature of *agape* is to share. The mother shares with her children to the point of self-denial because she loves. The God kind of love makes us want to share love with the unlovely, to reach out in forgiveness to the unforgiving, and to be merciful to the merciless. This is what makes it so incredible. Love makes the undeserving seem deserving to us, and we reach out to share ourselves with them.

God kind of sharing is also incredible since we want not only to share what we have, but also to share ourselves with others. It is not difficult to share some of what one has out of plenty. That is charity. What is amazing is the desire to share ourselves. That is solidarity. We stand in the midst of the poverty of the poor and feel their grinding dehumanization. We stand in the midst of the sinfulness of the sinful and feel their shame. We stand in the midst of the loneliness of the forgotten and forsaken and feel their throbbing hurt. This goes beyond just sharing and becomes bearing. He Himself bore our sins in His body on the cross" (1 Pet. 2:24). That alone spells out the lexicon of love that God wrote on that green hill far away.

It is interesting that in the poem of the Suffering Servant in Isaiah 53 the prophet Isaiah tells us that the Servant suffered personally for he was "a man of sorrows." He goes another step beyond that and says he suffered relatively for he bore our grief and carried our sorrows. He not only entered into the world as a human and as a human knew sorrow, but he actually carried the load of our guilt and shame. He did not pass up the bitter cup but drank its last dregs. The prophet takes us one step more and says that he suffered vicariously. He actually bore the penalty of separation from God. The prophet says, "It pleased the Lord to bruise him." Jesus fulfilled that prophecy as Suffering Servant when he cried, "My God, My God, why hast Thou forsaken me?" (Matt. 27:46). Jesus demonstrated *agape* love as caring, sharing, and bearing. He is our example. The church or the believer will never go beyond the ordinary in mission and missions without an adequate Christology. The missionary church has its vision of the missionary Christ intact.

God Is Love

The Son of God who entered this world on a mission as a missionary is a love-sent Son. The God of eternity, of creation, of redemption, and of revelation "was in Christ reconciling the world to Himself" (2 Cor. 5:19). God's attitude of love proceeds from his very nature for "God is love." Love is an eternal attitude of God, and it determines everything that God does in his ever working that those who were no people become the people of God (1 Pet. 2:10). The love of God provides the mission and the missionary with its imperative. God loved so much he sent his Missionary. We love so much we are missionaries. The church loves so much it sends its missionaries. Love not only sent our Savior to die in our place, but it also sends us to the person next door and to the people in the next town who have never heard.

Long before the Messiah came, God demonstrated his love for the world he made. Since God is love, his act of creation was an act of love. There is a risk in love because love makes one vulnerable. God made himself vulnerable in the creation of humanity. If we give love to another, they have the power to hurt us. If they leave you, you are lonely. If they say angry things to you, you are hurt. If they hit you, you cry. That is the constant risk we take in bearing children. They have enormous powers to make us happy or make us sad. In giving our love to them we are open to being hurt by them. As humans we have no way of knowing what our children will do to us. God, with his eyes wide open in his foreknowledge, knew the risk he was taking in making humans free. Because he loved, out of his own freedom he made humans in his image as free creatures.

The creation of human beings in the image of God is our greatest motive for missions and evangelism. Every man—pimp or potentate, prince or pauper, welfare recipient or worker, business executive or bandit—is made in his image. He created them for his glory to restore them to a right relationship to their Creator, to restore them to the glory of God. Missions is telling persons that they are made in his image to his glory. It is telling them that they are not the "naked ape" of evolution but "anthropos," human beings made in his image out of his love and for his glory. The text that has been called "the gospel in a nutshell" does not say that "God so loved nice people" that he gave his Son. It does not say that "God so loved church people" that He gave his only

Son. "God so loved the world that whosoever" makes it clear that he loves all human beings because he created all of us and is Father to all of us (Acts 17:28). The evaluation that God makes of all human beings is revealed in his love.

Jesus was seeking to tell men what the Heavenly Father was really like. In Luke 15 he is talking to religious leaders who really did not know that God is love. They were hard and rigid people. Their religion was as inflexible as they were. Salvation in their view was only for persons who kept their rules and worshiped exactly in their way. Everyone else would surely burn in hell. Jesus told them a story that we call "The Prodigal Son." It was the story of a father who gave his son everything. The son wasted it all. When the son had spent everything in wicked living, he decided to go home and work as one of his father's hired hands. To the son's surprise he found his father waiting for him. The father kissed him, and a great feast of celebration was held in honor of the returning son who "was lost and now is found." There is no mention of the word *love* in the parable but the story is about a father's love. Jesus was saying to the hypocritical religious leaders, "God is a loving, caring, sharing Father."

What is often forgotten about this story is that the prodigal in returning to the father discovered for the first time what it really meant to love the father. God is love and the response he wants from us is love. One of the most neglected passages that occurs in both Testaments is "You shall love the Lord your God with all your heart, and with all your soul, and with all your strength, and with all your mind; and your neighbor as yourself" (Luke 10:27). That passage is called "the great commandment." Perhaps in that passage more than any other biblical text the nature of *agape* is revealed. God kind of love can be commanded and it must therefore be more than an emotion. Emotional response cannot be commanded. It is not just a feeling. Feelings about persons cannot be commanded. God kind of love involves the heart, the soul, the body, the mind, and my relationships with other persons. Love is the commitment of the whole person to another. If that is the nature of a saving response to God, then it is imperative that the response is made clear in the life and commitment of the believer. The church is missionary not only in the verbalization of its message, but just as importantly in the incarnation of God kind of love.

The fact that God is love makes our response to radically love God critical for the missionary task. Another way of saying that we love God with a radical love is that we without question obey him. Jesus made this clear. "If ye love me, keep my commandments" (John 14:15, KJV). That clear statement came in the farewell discourses of Jesus with his disciples before his death. Judas, the betrayer, asked him a question as to how he was going to show himself to the world. Judas had been concerned about this. He wanted action. Jesus answered him by saying, "If a man love me, he will keep my words: and my Father will love him, (John 14:23, KJV). I will love him, and will manifest myself to him" (v. 21). Jesus was saying to Judas, "You are looking for me to set up a kingdom, to raise an army, and to conquer the world and get rid of the hated Romans. That is the way you want me to show myself. I am saying to you, Judas, that I am best shown to the world when you and all my disciples are obedient to what I have commanded. Love, Judas, and not worldly power is the evidence that I am from God. Now, if you want the world to know me, start putting into practice my words. Obey me, Judas, just obey me."

The critical factor in being a missionary, a missionary church, or a missionary denomination is obedience. If we love God, we will obey God. Paul quotes Isaiah 65, which is an indictment of Israel and uses the words "a disobedient people." The covenant with Abraham made it clear that Israel was to be a blessing to the nations. Israel failed as a missionary people. The Jews have never been a missionary people. They have difficulty understanding Christians at this very point. They do not understand why we try to lead persons to know God through Jesus Christ. They call our evangelism proselytizing. They do not understand because they have never been missionary. Some church members have the same problem. "Why do we send missionaries to people who already have religion?" It is a matter of obedience. God is love. To respond to him is to love him with body, soul, mind, and heart. Loving him like that demands implicit and unquestioning obedience. He told us to go to every city, every town, every village, and every rural place and share the God who is love with everyone. It is a matter of obedience. It is just as simple as that.

God's Love Incarnate

"God was in Christ reconciling the world to Himself" (2 Cor. 5:19). "The Word became flesh, and dwelt among us" (John 1:14). "Have this attitude in yourselves which was also in Christ Jesus, who, although He existed in the form of God, did not regard equality with God a thing to be grasped, but emptied Himself, taking the form of a bondservant, and being made in the likeness of men. And being found in appearance as a man, He humbled Himself by becoming obedient to the point of death, even death on the cross (Phil. 2:5-8). He was sent by the Father who "so loved the world." He came because he loved the Father and was obedient to him.

Thomas on one occasion responded to what Jesus was saying about his going to the Father and preparing a place for the disciples. Jesus said they knew what he was saying because they knew where he was going and they knew the way. Thomas blurted out that he certainly did not know where Jesus was going and he did not know the way. Then, Jesus made his great claim that he was the Way, the Truth, and the Life and that access to the Father is through him. Then Phillip said to Jesus, "Show us the Father, and it is enough for us. Jesus said to him, 'Have I been so long with you, and yet you have not come to know Me, Philip? He who has seen me has seen the Father; how do you say: 'Show us the Father'?" (John 14:8-9).

Jesus Christ is love, revealing the Father who is love. We know the Father when we know him. "God, after He spoke long ago to the fathers in the prophets in many portions and in many ways, in these last days has spoken to us in His Son, whom He appointed heir of all things, through whom also He made the world. And He is the radiance of His glory and the exact representation of His nature, and upholds all things by the word of His power" (Heb. 1:1-3). As the incarnation of God, Jesus was love—love sent, love being, and love revealing. The name that Jesus most used about himself was "the Son of Man." Cicero will always be known to us as the Roman. Aristotle will always be known to us as the Greek. Kant will always be known to us as the German. Jesus Christ alone is known to us as "the Son of Man." His love makes him stand in solidarity with the whole race. The love that sends the missionary is color, class, and culture blind. The missionary is blind in the same way.

Jesus Christ is the love of God thinking. Literally, Philippians 2:5 says, "Have this mind-set in yourselves which was also in Christ Jesus." It is amazing how much the New Testament deals with the mind renewed in Christ. We usually think about other aspects of transformation that Christ works in us. The New Testament is clear that the thinking of a Christian is radically changed by Christ. The call of Paul for the Romans to give to God their bodies as a living and holy sacrifice is often quoted and exposited but the "be transformed by the renewing of our mind" is usually neglected (Rom. 12:1-2). How we think about things is often more determined by our culture than by the Bible and Christ's example. The whole burden of Philippians 2 is that the Christians mind has an attitude of unselfishness. It is always thinking about others and not self. The way we think determines how missionary we are and how missionary the church is. If we do our thinking in terms of race, color, or class, we will not stand for the solidarity of the human race.

Our missionary sociology should come from Jesus Christ and not our culture. In relation to Jesus Christ there is only one gospel, one race, and one task. The commonality of all the race is found in its relationship to Jesus Christ. All persons are sinners because they have rejected the light of the world. All persons can be saved by accepting God's Messiah, Jesus, as Lord and

Savior. Jesus had an attitude of love toward the poor, the sick, the retarded, the insane, and the sinners. We cannot pick and choose the objects of our missionary concern. We must go where God is working and where his Spirit opens doors of opportunity. The most scathing denunciations of Jesus were reserved for the racism of the Pharisees who were blind to the plight of the poor, the wretchedness of the leper, the alienation of the Samaritans, and the rejection of the woman taken in adultery.

Jesus Christ is the love of God acting. The God kind of love was incarnate in every act of Jesus of Nazareth. He stood in the frontiers of poverty, disease, and death as the love of God in action. Acting contrary to custom and culture he challenged demonic powers and human enemies to touch the leper with healing, to touch the insane with sanity, and to touch the poor with food, comfort and hope. Annie Johnson Flint, inspired by the raising of the daughter of Jairus in Mark 5:35-42, wrote the following lines that show how his presence often makes the difference:

> There were six in the room where death had been;
>   The little dead maid was one,
> Two were the parents with broken hearts
>   For all they could do was done;
>
> Three were the pitying men who came
>   To the house where the dead child lay;
> And death was stronger than all of them,
>   For death had had his way.
>
> The power of man and the strength of man,
>   Were vain to help or save,
> And the mother-love could not restore
>   The life that once she gave.
>
> But Life had followed the feet of Death
>   To banish man's despair.
> And the child came back from the gates of the grave;
>   There were six, and Jesus there.[2]

If we want to know what we ought to do in responding to the missionary imperative, why don't we do what he did? He did not need a computer to work out where the "soft spots" were in culture that would most quickly respond to the gospel. He found the soft spots in tear-stained faces, hungry stomachs, and running sores. He found need in the guilt of an adulterous woman, the pride of a Pharisee, and the writhing body of an epileptic. He acted naturally, instantaneously, and lovingly to human need. He even went as a guest to the home of a Pharisee where he would be insulted in order to meet a fallen woman whose name he made a memorial wherever the gospel is preached. He often went against the grain of what was "nice" or customary or religious in order to meet human need. We are not like him when we are repelled by sinners rather than attracted to them.

Jesus Christ is the God kind of love dying. He said that He did not come into the world to be ministered to but to minister and give his life (Matt. 20:28). That was the final price the world exacted from One who utterly loved. We could not stand him for he reminded us too much of what we are not. The one who conquered hate by loving, strife by peacemaking, hurt by touching, and injury by healing on the cross conquers death by dying. The love that made him minister led him to his death. When we stand at Calvary, we can only sing, "No greater love." In the last agonies of death he utters those words of love that can never be forgotten by all who love him, "Father, forgive them; for they do not know what they are doing" (Luke 23:34). The cross is the symbol of our mission and his. The missionary meaning of that cross is self-denial to the point of the "I" dying that "he" may live. Amy Carmichael has caught that spirit of death to self in her poem "Self-Discipline":

> When I look up and triumph over every sinful thing,
> The things that no one knows about, the cowardly selfish thing,
> And when with heart and will I live to please my glorious King,
> That is discipline.
> To trample on that glorious thing inside of me that says, "I,"
> To think of others, always, never, never of that "I,"
> To learn to live according to my Savior's word, "Deny,"
> That is discipline.

The Continuing Incarnation of Love

Do you think that Zacchaeus ever forgot that day when he climbed down out of that tree and led Jesus to his home? Do you think Nicodemus ever forgot that night when he blew out the lamp, closed the door, and went to the house where Jesus was staying? Do you think the woman at the well ever forgot that noonday when she came to know Jesus of Nazareth at the well of Samaria? Do you think that the four fisherman ever forgot that morning when they left their nets hanging in the sun and their boat by the seaside to follow Jesus down many dusty roads and into many obscure villages? They could never forget because after that they were never the same. He came into their lives and they began the experience of growing into his likeness. They began that process of dying to self from the moment they came to know him. He would leave them and give them his mission to complete.

Paul, in the letters to the Ephesians and Colossians, exposits the church as the body, the continuing incarnation of Jesus Christ. Jesus had promised that after he was gone that they would do greater things than he had done. The promise is given to the Christian and to the church. "Truly, truly, I say to you, he who believes in Me, the works that I do shall he do also; and greater works than these shall he do; because I go to the Father" (John 14:12). The Word is made flesh in the believer. The Word is "God is love." The Word is that God's love was incarnate in Jesus of Nazareth. The Word is that God's love that was incarnate in Jesus of Nazareth is now incarnate in the believer and in the church. That word of love must become love incarnate in us. That love incarnate must touch, comfort, cheer, and bring hope where people hurt, where people mourn, where hope is gone, and where injury is given.

We must take Christ out of the cloisters of the monastery and the church, out from behind the stained glass and organ preludes, out from behind the barriers of a holy mumbo jumbo that no one understands. We must take him out where persons live and die, swear and bless, sweat and toil. We must take him out in us. We must take him to the community, the state, and the nation. He must become incarnate in the halls of justice and legislation, in the world of trade and commerce, in the plush executive offices of the world of banking and speculation, in the ghettos of poverty and the jungle of crime and unemployment, in the swank suburbs and the blighted inner cities. We need missionaries where no mission board can send missionaries. We need to make Christ come alive in the world of people. The only possibility that this will be true will lie with our ability to incarnate Christ in the marketplace.

Can you ever forget the night, the morning, or the day when you came to him and he came to you? Have you ever been the same since? Is what he began in you growing more and more into his likeness? The missionary vision is that the kingdoms of this world sill become the kingdom of our God and his Christ. That is the dream to which the Christian is committed. The fulfillment of that vision waits on our incarnation of Christ in being God kind of love, thinking God kind of love, and acting God kind of love. He wants to go out on the city streets and mix and mingle with the crowds of irreligious because he loves them, but he will never go on the streets of your city unless you go there. He wants to go into the homes of the poor, the suffering, and the sinful, but he will never go to those homes unless you go there. He wants to go into the plush offices and talk to the executive who has lost himself and God in the corporate rat race, but he will never go there unless you go there.

When you go, he will be going. When you love, he will be loving. When you pray, he will be praying. You are a missionary. When you say to them, "I love you," and show them your love in your attitudes and acts they will know that you have been with him. The fragrance of his life will be upon you. The aura of his love will be about you. In his name the lonely will laugh again, the cheerless will smile again, the hurt will stop their crying and the tormented will sit down quietly and listen to you because you are a missionary. *Agape*, the God kind of love, is a clue to the very nature of God. It is an explanation of our Lord's life and ministry. It is the driving power of the missionary's mission and message. We have to say with a great preacher of years ago, "Love is the greatest thing in the world." We have to say with Paul, "But now abide faith, hope, love, these three; but the greatest of these is love" (1 Cor. 13:13).

Notes

1. William Owen Carver, *Missions in the Plan of the Ages* (Nashville; Broadman, 1951), p. 11

2. Flint, *Poems*, Vol. 2, p. 133.

9

Our Mission to America

Breathes there a man with soul so dead,
who never to himself hath said,
"This is my own, my native land!"

SIR WALTER SCOTT

Every Jew remembers with pride Ha Eretz Israel. Moses was no exception. He is a classic example of the believer-patriot. He saw with clear eyes both the strengths and the weaknesses of his nation. His farewell speech delivered to Israel just before his death ranks with Lincoln's Gettysburg Address, the speech of Churchill to the English-speaking peoples of the world, and Washington's Farewell to his troups. The speech burns with the passion and fervor of the prophet-patriot. It pulsates with love for God and love for country. Verses 7-14 of Deuteronomy 8 are particularly appealing:

For the Lord your God is bringing you into a good land, a land of brooks of water, of fountains and springs, flowing forth in valleys and hills; a land of wheat and barley, of vines and fig trees and pomegranates, a land of olive oil and honey; a land where you shall eat food without scarcity, in which you shall not lack anything; a land whose stones are iron, and out of whose hills you can dig copper. When you have eaten and are satisfied, you shall bless the Lord your God for the good land which He has given you. Beware lest you forget the Lord your God by not keeping His commandments and His ordinances and His statutes, which I am commanding you today; lest . . . you forget the Lord your God who brought you out from the land of Egypt.

The prophet-patriot sees clearly the sins of today that bring the judgment of tomorrow. He warns this nomadic people about to become a nation that there are three fatal mistakes they can make. He tells them that they can miss the lessons of their history. For this reason this nation was committed to passing down the oral tradition of their history from father to son in the liturgy of the Passover. He warns them that they can miss the meaning of their prosperity. Prosperity can cause them to swell with pride and forget God. Finally he warns them not to miss the threat of their enemies. The real enemies, he tells them, are not from the outside but on the inside. Unbelief and idolatry are the sins that will eat away at the crumbling foundations of freedom. Without falling into the error of civil religion, we do well to remind ourselves that these fatal mistakes are the Achilles' heel of all civilizations.

The title of this chapter, like the speech of Moses, mixes the magic of two great words. With Moses it is "God" and "country." Our title mixes the magic of "mission" and "America." With us, as with Moses, it is not a case of standing for everything our nation stands for, but we do stand up for our country. Not everything our country does is right, but we do love our country, right or wrong. Our title really mixes the magic of three words, "America," "mission," and "our."

"America" is Jerry Clower, Charlie Pride, Van Cliburn, Phyllis Diller, and Bob Hope. America is pizza, popcorn, hamburgers hot dogs, and tacos. America is the Kentucky Derby, the Indianapolis 500, the World Series, and the Superbowl. America is the Declaration of Independence, the Constitution, and the Bill of Rights. America is Billy Graham, Oral Roberts, and Rex Humbard. America is swanky hotels and sleazy massage parlors. America is beautifully manicured suburbs and vermin-infested slums. America is sailboats, automobiles, motorcycles, and airplanes. America is discotheques, cathedrals, museums, and homosexual bars. America is *Dallas, Soap, The Waltons, The Muppets,* and *Buck Rogers.* America is Nat King Cole, Elvis Presley, and Bing Crosby. America is McKinley standing like a crystal king amid the winter wonderland of Alaska. America is Haleakala, "the house of the sun," whose shadow at sunrise extends a thousand miles into the blue waters of the Pacific.

America is a dream of liberty, equality, and equal justice for
all. America is a nightmare of alcoholism, drugs, pornography,
and injustice. America is everything good that can bless people in
genuine self-realization and happiness. America is everything
evil that can destroy people, ruining character and principles.
America is greed and self-denial, racism and openness, hate and
love, the divine and the demonic, the good and the bad all
mixed up in a mosaic of agony and ecstasy.

"Mission" is also a magic word. Mission in media is the *Star-
ship Enterprise*, *Hill Street Blues*, and *Charlie's Angels*. Mission
in history is Columbus and Cortez, Byrd and Lindbergh, John
Glenn and Buzz Aldrin. Mission in space is *Gemini, Apollo*, the
Viking, and the *Eagle*. Mission in Christian history is Ma Slessor,
David Livingstone, Luther Rice, William Bagby, and Annie Arm-
strong. Mission in medicine is Hippocrates, Galen, William
Harvey, Henry Gray, Louis Pasteur, Joseph Lister, and Jonas
Salk. Mission in art is Leonardo da Vinci. Mission in science is
Aristotle, Newton, Einstein, Max Planck, and Niels Bohr. Mis-
sion in inventive genius is Gutenberg, McCormick, Edison, and
Ford.

Mission in Home Missions is Russel Holman, William McIn-
tosh, Isaac Tichenor, Courts Redford, and Arthur Rutledge. Mission for Home Missions is evangelism, career missionaries,
US-2ers, Sojourners, Mission Service Corps Volunteers, and
mission consultants. Mission in the local church is Cooperative
Program, Lottie Moon, Annie Armstrong, mission Sunday
Schools, personal evangelism, satellite churches, and lay
evangelism schools. Mission in the Christian faith is incarnation:
"God was in Christ reconciling the world to Himself" (2 Cor.
5:19).

"Our" is a personal word. It is Southern Baptists. It is you and
I. It is "our" mission to America. It does not ignore the heroic and
sacrificial mission of other Christian groups to evangelize this nation, but it focuses on our task, our responsibility, our mission. It
is 13,000,000 plus Southern Baptists, 35,000 Southern Baptist
churches, 34,000 Southern Baptist pastors. It is wealth, prop-

erty, people, and leadership. It is an unbelievable potential of the largest and richest body of evangelicals in America. "Our" is a word of cooperation as "workers together with God" we match the resources of money, persons, and spiritual gifts to the needs for evangelistic, social, and mission ministries to a spiritually needy nation.

"Our" is a word of responsibility for the evangelization of our country, the good and the bad, the affluent and the poor, the cultured and the crude. They are our responsibility that we can neither evade nor avoid. Since 1845, our mission to America has been focused in the Home Mission Board. It is our task to assist churches in taking the gospel from those who know Christ to those who do not know him. Our mission is to go to places that churches cannot go with the reconciling message. It is our task to assist churches in planting other churches within the reach of every person in this land. Pastors and churches have a right to know how we perceive our mission to America. You have a right to know our theological commitment, our biblical concerns, and our personal commitment. The task is our task—every last one of us. It begins where you live and extends to Puerto Rico on the east, to Samoa on the west, to the Florida Keys on the south, and to Kotzebue, Alaska, on the north.

Our Theological Commitment

We are committed to the fact that the God of creation, the Father of us all, has chosen to reveal himself to us in the Bible and in Jesus Christ. He is the God who has spoken to us by the fathers and by Jesus Christ. He is known to us as Father, Son, and Holy Spirit. We are committed to the life-changing, mind-blowing power of the gospel to save. We firmly believe it to be "the power of God unto salvation" (Rom. 1:16). It is the good news of God, of Jesus Christ, of the grace of God, of the kingdom of God, and the good news of your salvation. We believe that there is a distilled essence of the gospel with which there is no compromise. We have a message that is not to be tampered with, revised, or rethought. It must be communicated, not changed. We believe it must be communicated faithfully in the vocabulary and concepts of a modern world.

We are committed to the redeeming love of God for his world and therefore for our nation. We believe that the Bible and the incarnation demonstrate that God is in love with this confused nation whose people wander in midday as if it were midnight lost in all the cul-de-sac of prosperity, pleasure, and position. God distilled that love for us on a skull-shaped hill outside of Jerusalem long ago in a bloody man on a cross. John 3:16 is the focus, and "the world" is the circumference of that task. In thinking of ourselves as a continuing base in the United States for our world mission, we need to remember that we cannot take to the world what we have not been able to do in our own nation. It is difficult for the nations of the world to understand that we want to export something to other countries that we have not been able to work at home. This makes our mission to America imperative.

God loves this land from the Aleutian Islands to the Florida Keys, from International Falls, Minnesota, to Harlingen, Texas. Jesus Christ did not sort out while he was here whom he was going to love and whom he wasn't going to love. He did not classify persons by race or color or economic status. If he had a preference, it was for the disinherited and disenchanted. Even the crucifiers were not thought to be impossible for the grace of God for he prayed, "Father forgive them; for they do not know what they are doing" (Luke 23:34). We have every reason to believe that if he returned again as he did the first time that we would not find him at some denominational institution. We would probably find him in what we call the slums or the ghettos of poverty and want, holding little children and cuddling them.

God loves the blighted inner cities that we have allowed to become jungles of unemployment, crime, and drug addiction. God loves the junkies, the pimps, the prostitutes, the homosexuals, and the mainliners. God loves the concrete jungles of our great cities which have become a montage of magnificence and misery, of plenty and poverty, of nudity and nobility, of power and oppression. Paul Tillich pointed out that God is man's ultimate concern, but from the viewpoint of the Bible and the incarnation man is God's ultimate concern. Our mission to America demands that we stand upon the distillation of the Christian message into its ultimate essence—we care. We care because he taught us to care and because caring is what the gospel leaves with us. He showed us what caring means.

We recognize the exceeding sinfulness of sin. "Whatever happened to sin?" is a good question for us as well as for a great psychiatrist. The sinfulness of man is the only sufficient explanation for the demonic in man and in all that man does. Philosophies and idealogies that have no doctrine of sin are hard pressed to explain our predicament. We have a way of blaming others and even God for the messes we get our lives into. "I made a blunder," "I pulled a boo-boo," "I made a mistake," are all very easy to say, but the hardest words for men, societies, and nations to say are, "I have sinned."

Arthur Miller in his stage play, *The Creation of the World and Other Business*, imagines a dialogue between God and the devil. God comes in the room where Lucifer is standing in front of a mirror posing himself and obviously admiring what he sees. Lucifer brushes back a stray lock of hair, flicks imaginary specks from his clothing. God watches Lucifer preening himself like a vain peacock for a time and then says, "Aha, admiring yourself again! Don't you know that is the very thing that got you in trouble in the first place?" Lucifer turns around and says, "I am just admiring what you made, Lord!" It is the same old canard we have been pulling on ourselves and God since Eden, "You made me like I am, and I can't help it." God didn't make us like we are, and we can help it.

Sin has billowed every graveyard and peopled every asylum. Sin has broken every heart and troubled every life at one time or another. No physician, no matter how skilled in material medicine, can prescribe for that illness. No surgeon, no matter how deft his hands, can cut away that malignancy. No psychiatrist, no matter how perceptive, can talk that cleavage out of one's personality. We take seriously the seriousness of sin. The fruit of sin is drunkenness, drug addiction, murder, adultery, stealing, lying, and all the other crimes, perversions, and problems. The root is sin—alienation from God—estrangement from the love of God—separation from the Holy Sinless One. We are sinners, by nature, by birth, and by practice. We do not need a reformation or a readjustment, but a resurrection. We need the coming alive of the spiritual being we are, made in the image of God. Only God can do that. That transformation is so radical, so revolutionary, and so revelatory that we can only describe it as the Bible describes it. It is a "new birth."

This is the heart of what our mission task is about in this nation. We have at the Home Mission Board a Department of Social Ministries, and I believe that Christian social ministry is one of the prime expressions of our evangelistic and missionary concern. We also have a Department of Interfaith Witness, and I believe dialogue is a vital expression of our evangelism. However, none of us believes that "a cup of cold water" or an hour's conversation is a substitute for Jesus Christ. What is wrong with persons is something that only God can set straight. It is our mission to tell this land that Jesus Christ is the answer. We intend to tell them that there is a balm in Gilead. What God has said and done in his revelation of himself in the Bible and in Jesus Christ is our message. To spread this good news we plant churches and proclaim that saving word.

One can really take sin seriously when one sees sin from the viewpoint of Calvary. When we see that wounded Man on a cross and know that the sinless is dying for the sinful, the lovely for the unlovely, the pure for the defiled, then we come to understand the relationship between sin and suffering.

Our Biblical Concerns

W. O. Carver was without question the greatest missiologist Southern Baptists had ever produced. His vision of our world mission was breathtakingly Pauline. In his matchless paraphrase of Ephesians, he made the church a very significant essential of the gospel. Paul sees his task as not only preaching to the Gentiles the "unsearchable riches of Christ" but also as "helping all the races of men to see what is the fellowship of the mystery." There is more than the continuing affirmation of the creative and dynamic reality of the gospel in all of its timely and timeless applications; also there is the enlisting of participants in the Master's global mission. Our biblical concerns must go beyond simplistic interpretations of the gospel. If God is present in his world, in his church, and his Spirit, then we must take seriously God's plan. The Phillips translation makes this plan for Bold Mission clear. "For God has allowed us to know the secret of his plan, and it is this: he purposed long ago in his sovereign will that all human history should be consummated in Christ, that everything that exists in Heaven or earth should find its perfection and fulfilment in him" (Eph. 1:9-10).

Gerald Anderson, the Methodist missiologist, says that the first task in reaching out in mission to the world is that "you have to begin by understanding the world, and loving the world—as God loves it."[1] It would seem then that a very important biblical concern is that we learn how to love this nation before we try to win it to Christ. This is much deeper than patriotic devotion or nostalgic longing for the America that once was—rural and tranquil. It means loving all of this nation just as it is. Loving the cities with their aggravated problems of crime, unemployment, and poverty will be a good place of beginning. Loving the people with all their ethnic, religious, and cultural distinctives is a good place to continue our loving. God loves his world. This is a biblical axiom. This truth is burned more deeply on the pages of the Bible and in the face of Jesus Christ than any other message.

Because God is love, he has opted to reveal himself to us in the context of history. Because God is love, he has opted to reveal himself to us in the context of the history of our nation. The incarnation is made real to those outside of Christ when the God who is love is incarnate in us. When we love others, the message of God's love incarnate in Christ is more easily communicated. Our caring love makes us want to give every person an opportunity to hear the gospel and to give every person the opportunity of becoming a part of a caring, loving fellowship. That is "the fellowship of the mystery."

Hugo Culpepper has defined the mission of the church for us. He says, "The *mission* of the church is to glorify God by leading persons to know him through faith in Jesus Christ."[2] Evangelism is at the heart of the mission of the church. The church is mission, and the mission is to lead persons to know God through Jesus Christ and so experience his love. It is not an accident that the first guideline for the work of the Home Mission Board is evangelism. The only goal that is as big as the love of God is the goal that every person should hear the gospel and have opportunity to respond to it with faith. We do have caring love for the more than 85 million persons outside of Christ in the United States. We believe that this concern for those out of Christ is both biblical and Christlike.

"If we care, we share." Those words are more than a slogan for a charitable fund drive. They are reflections of the whole life of Christ. The early church was a witnessing church. The more than 85 million persons in the United States who are not Christians must be evangelized. That responsibility involves an impossible undertaking if our evangelism is confined to the preaching ministry of our 35,000 churches. The undertaking is not impossible if every Southern Baptist is motivated, equipped, and trained for personal evangelism. A major strategy of the Evangelism Section of the Home Mission Board is to assist churches to accomplish this goal. John Havlik, in *The Evangelistic Church*, points out this faith-sharing aspect of the life and work of the church:

The church that shares its faith is a church that finds one point of commonality—Jesus Christ. We may be very diverse racially, socially, economically, but the overriding point of contact is the called out people of God. They are called out from Jew and Gentile to become the new race of men, the new social order—the church. This is the faith that binds us together. This is the faith we share. We must share our faith with one another before we can share it with the world.[3]

We have another biblical concern. Not many years ago Southern Baptists planted a church in Tolland, Connecticut, where Shubal Stearns was awakened by the "new light" that gave birth to the Separate Baptists. He brought the awakening for Baptists to Virginia where he was ill-treated by the establishment. He and his brother-in-law, Daniel Marshall, came to Sandy Creek in Guilford County, North Carolina, and established the great Sandy Creek Baptist Church. That church was responsible for planting a string of churches from Chesapeake Bay to Georgia and from the Atlantic to the Kentucky frontier. Morgan Edwards, in *History of North Carolina Baptists*, says that this church "is the mother of all Separate Baptists." That church without any denominational agencies to assist and without any formally educated clergy and without the benefits of a modern transportation system set a precedent for us in planting, nurturing, and building new churches.

We are the children of mighty sires. That heroic band of seventeen has given us an example in sacrifice and devotion that should inspire us to this day. There are still more than 500 counties that we need to enter. There are still many large cities barely penetrated. Courts Redford in the fifties said that one of the most important reasons for the success of Southern Baptists at a time when we were growing five times as fast as the population was the planting of "church type missions." We have become surfeited with success. We have become fat, lazy, and contented. We have not responded to the stimuli of the Spirit in the voice of "the man from Macedonia." The cry, "Come over and help us," no longer stirs us into action. The spirit of the pioneer that has to cross the next range of mountains simply because it is there is gone from many of our churches. We need a fresh infusion of the spirit of missions.

It is not a matter of agency policy and loads of money. It is the Spirit that makes a church go to the other neighborhood, the next town, the adjacent county, and even into another state to plant a church for the glory of God. Our current goal to put an evangelical, warm, evangelistic church within the reach of every person in the United States in this century is not unrealistic. By the year 2000 this can be a reality if our churches will listen to the Holy Spirit's missionary call. We must hear "the voices of missions" again. Once more in our history we must be thrilled by the opportunities God has given us as the largest group of evangelicals in this nation.

Our Personal Commitment

After his experience on the field, a US-2 missionary of the Home Mission Board wrote words that indicate the kind of response that will make us feel what we must feel and be what we must be in our mission to America:

> I thought of crying
>   until I saw another's tears—
> I felt the pangs of loneliness
>   until I saw another's isolation—
> I thought of being defeated
>   until the broken life stumbled by—
> I felt the strain of fatigue
>   until I saw the restless face.
> I must be truth
>   with a cloth to dry the tears—
> I must be light
>   with a visit to the lonely—
> I must be word
>   with a hope for a better day—
> I must be love
>   with a concern for all men.
> I must be. . . .

The young missionary poet ended that poem with the words, "I must be" and a long ellipsis. He did not know what he must be tomorrow when it comes with its new challenges and new opportunities. He knew we would read what he had written, and he was not daring to tell us what we must be in the light of our challenges and our opportunities.

Our personal commitment is to Christ. If the words ". . . inasmuch as ye have done it unto one of the least of these my brethren, ye have done it unto me . . ." (KJV) means anything, they mean that the only way we can express our love for him and commitment to him is to share his love with others and make a commitment to others. There are millions out there who find hope impossible, love scarce, and faith difficult. His whole ministry and all of his words focus with pinpoint particularity upon those who hurt—who are battered and beaten by life. We are committed to being the good news to them and sharing the good news with them until everyone has heard and everyone has opportunity to share in a caring community of Christians. We are committed to helping them to understand that faith, hope, and love are as real as life and as near to them as Jesus Christ. We intend to tell every person that he is not an orphan weeping in vain on the bony shoulder of despair, but that he is a child of God and that the Father knows, cares, and is willing to save to the uttermost.

The struggle is for the soul, the life of America. Who shall have America? Christ or Satan? Who shall have the brains of our universities? Who shall have the genius of our industry? Who shall have the storied bounty of our prairies? Who shall have the ingenuity of our scientific communities? Who shall have the rich treasures still buried in our mountains? Who shall have the precious people of this nation? An American churchman tells of visiting Poland soon after the holocaust of World War II. He asked a Polish Christian, "Who shall have Poland after the war, Christ or communism?" The Pole answered with deep emotion, "Whichever makes its message a flame of fire." Our success in evangelizing this nation will depend on the depth of our commitment. Mission is giving ourselves without reservation to promote what we believe are ultimate and supreme concerns.

There is a recurring and insistent need for commitment to our mission to America. There is a need for thousands of young people to make a commitment with a determination to prepare themselves for a career in Home Missions. There is a need for hundreds of young people to discover on the field the glory and the grime of the mission field by making a commitment to serve one or two years between college and seminary as a US-2 missionary. There is a need for a million volunteers who find their own support in Home Missions to support and supplement the work of career missionaries. During the Second World War, there were posters everywhere with Uncle Sam pointing a long, bony finger right out of the picture. The caption read, "Uncle Sam wants you." Jesus Christ wants you. Are you ready to make a commitment to him?

Notes

1. Arthur L. Walker, Jr., ed., *Educating for Christian Missions* (Nashville: Broadman, 1981), p. 49.
2. Ibid., p. 42.
3. John Havlik, *The Evangelistic Church* (Nashville: Convention Press, 1976), p. 36.